MW01294091

SPRINTING THROUGH SETBACKS

AN OLYMPIAN'S GUIDE TO OVERCOMING SELF-DOUBT AND IMPOSTER SYNDROME

MICHA POWELL

WITH

MOLLY HURFORD

CONTENTS

Sprinting Through Setbacks: An Olympian's Guide to Overcoming Self-Doubt and Imposter Syndrome
Copyright © 2024 by Micha Powell with Molly Hurford
All rights reserved. This book or any portion thereof may not be reproduced or used in any manner whatsoever without the express written permission of the publisher except for the use of brief quotations in a book review.

978-1-7782057-9-8

First edition, 2024

More Information: StrongGirlPublishing.com

To all the people who have helped me become the athlete that I am today

And especially to my mom,
who helped me embrace the uncertainty of greatness

FOREWORD

BY ROSEY UGOCHUKWU EDEH, OLYMPIAN

In her career so far, Micha Powell has experienced incredible athletic highs and some soul-searching sporting disappointments. The fact that Micha was born to two Olympic parents, one with a world record and one with a Canadian record, did very little to make her athletic journey easy. In fact, Micha was dotted with self-doubt due in part to that very fact.

As Micha's mom, I have taught her from a super young age to learn from your disappointments. Micha took that advice to heart. Back in the early 2000s, Micha was sweating it out in one of her first ever youth soccer games and suddenly she got a soccer ball square in the face. There's a bit of blood trickling from her nose, but her coach gets her a towel, she's cleaned up and a few minutes later she's back out on the pitch playing with her team. After the game, it was popsicles and smiles for everyone, including Micha.

Allow me to shine more light on Micha's "I will" attitude:

Writing a memoir before the age of 30? The evidence is on the pages of this very book!

Another example, while watching Usain Bolt blaze to Olympic glory at the 2012 London Olympics on TV and having never raced on a track before, she says, "Mom! Let's go to the track across the street. I need you to time my 100 meters, okay?"

"Okay," I said. Her time was pretty decent for testing her wheels out on a rock-hard asphalt track. Spurred on by her results, she signs up for cross-country a couple of months later during her final year at Leaside High School and helps the team win the City Championships and makes it to the Ontario Federation of School Athletic Associations (OFSAA) Cross Country Finals that same year. Following her cross-country exploits, she goes on to qualify and compete at her first OFSAA track championships and runs away with a silver in the 400 meters.

One more! This time I'm going way back to five-year-old Micha, who comes to the defence of a classmate and now great friend in the schoolyard during recess. I'm not trying to promote physical altercations, but my little girl saw her friend being bullied and took that bully to task. She was punished and had to spend time at "the wall." When I picked her up from school and asked how her day was, she proudly announced that she stood up for a friend being teased by a bigger kid. She said, ever so defiantly and without a sliver of regret, "I'm glad I stood up for my friend, maman."

Micha's memoir takes the reader through several pivotal races in her still-evolving track career, offering a large window into the world of high performance athletics and high stakes mental growth. Any reader who's experienced doubt, Imposter Syndrome and stress, you're not alone. So has Micha. The life lessons and emotional growth Micha has experienced through the toughest sprint distance on the track reveal important keys to overcoming setbacks and embracing success. Read on and you'll find out what they are.

-Rosey Ugochukwu Edeh

INTRODUCTION

Being a professional athlete might seem like a series of goals you achieve, but in reality, it's more like a series of setbacks that you have to navigate constantly, and those who can sprint through their setbacks and move on to the next thing are the ones who thrive. It's about being able to constantly assess where you are, figure out what you can control, chart a new course, and follow through on the execution. Repeat as needed.

Racing the 400-meter is a good metaphor for tackling pretty much anything in your life, whether it's a big project for school or work, or if you're like me and you race on the track. The 400 requires precision training, being able to break down a hard effort into manageable chunks, and being able to execute on the day, with no excuses. And then, you go out and do it again and again and again.

It's a race that requires a lot of raw power, but it's also a long event for a sprinter and it requires a certain amount of tactics in addition to just "running fast." A well-executed 400-meter race breaks down into four parts. In the first 100 meters, you're trying to go out as hard as you can. You're using that bit of stored energy that's like lighting a match—but it burns out quickly and then your body switches over to a different energy system. In that short window, you want to use the flame to get up to your top speed. In your second 100 meters of the race, you're trying to hold that momentum and speed. You're getting into a fast but relaxed feeling, and you're telling your body that you're almost to the halfway mark. In the third 100 meters, you're thinking, 'Okay, I've got to make a move.' If you hold off any longer, your body is going to be telling you to stop, and it's not going to be able to do anything. It's time to go. You can't *actually* go any faster at that point, you've already reached your maximum. But there's a feeling that you're willing to push a little bit more. In that last turn, you're gathering your momentum. And if you've done it right, you've put yourself in a great position, if you've used your energy efficiently, now it's the last 100. In the last 100, let's be honest, it's about whoever can run the least slow. It's not about who can run the fastest, there's nobody truly sprinting the last 100, you can't physically do that.

The winner is the person who doesn't get caught up in what other people are doing. She's the one who's out there running with the greatest sense of purpose. When you see the finish, you look past the line and you *charge*.

I believe that your best results don't come from the day when you're at a big meet. They're built when you're training and when you're telling yourself that you want to be the best athlete you can be. That means being the most prepared, coming into a race with the strongest mindset and being the most focused. That effort every day is what makes any of these titles—Olympian, record holder, gold medalist—have more weight.

In this book, I'm looking back at 11 of the pivotal races in my career so far. They're not all my best results—far from it, in some cases—but each one was a turning point, a moment of learning for me.

I've been racing since I was 17, but despite having two parents who were Olympic track runners, I wasn't always a runner. I actually wanted to be a tennis player since the moment I saw Serena Williams step onto the court. But running was in my DNA, and by the time I hit my teen years, it demanded my attention. I fell in love with the 400-meter race late in high school and never looked back.

Since then, I've raced at the highest collegiate level and for the Canadian National Team. I have a gold medal from the Commonwealth Games and was part of the 4x400-meter relay team for the Rio Olympics. My career has had its highs and its lows, and I've learned a lot about what it means to go as hard as humanly possible for under a minute... and I've learned just how long that minute can start to feel!

In international meets, people recognize me because they know my parents. I am reminded all the time about my dad or my mom. In one way, it feels really special to be part of the community, this next generation of athletes. I'm literally continuing on their legacy. But getting introduced on the microphone as Mike Powell's daughter, not as me? That feels less good. They're not bringing up my accomplishments or talking about me as being my own person who's creating my own legacy—in those moments, I feel like I'm just the extension of their legacy. I'm proud to be their daughter, but I'm also proud to be a runner in my own right.

Even with stellar results as a runner, it's tough for me not to compare myself to my parents—especially when racing on the world stage. Both of my parents have been in the Olympics multiple times. They make it seem like that's just something you do. And that has admittedly messed up my perception, especially when I made the Rio team in 2016, didn't race in that Olympic Games, and then didn't make the Tokyo Games in 2021. Making one Olympic team should have been a huge deal, a major accomplishment. But because neither of my parents stopped at one team, I felt like one wasn't enough.

This book, like my running, is my chance to blaze my own path. And it's not one that has been simple or easy. For every two steps forward, there was a step back—sometimes a really big step back! For any good race or record broken, there was a question in my head about what was next. For every announcer who talked about me and my accomplishments, there was an announcer who mispronounced my name or only talked about my parents' accomplishments. For every person who made me feel as though I belonged, there was someone who was questioning that, questioning me.

On the track, you often hear about somebody who's a high school phenom, and then they keep that trajectory going, turn pro, and it's a straightforward career. For me, I had slow growth in small spurts. If you were paying close attention, you may have thought I had potential, but it wasn't in your face. I was good, but I was surrounded by greats in my peers and my parents. From day one, I had impostor syndrome, always asking, 'Am I really good?' And any result I did get, I'd question: 'Is this a fluke?'

Writing this while navigating not just Olympic qualifications but also dealing with an injury has been hard. How much do you talk about Paris 2024 throughout the book if it's not a sure thing? But not talking about it... it's the goal, the reason I'm training, the reason I'm putting in the work. To *not* talk about it just because I may not make the team would feel like I'm lying to you all about my motivations. So as this goes to print, I don't know if I'm going to Paris. But I do know that if I didn't speak (or write) that goal into the world, it definitely wouldn't be happening. Will I be okay if I don't make it? Absolutely. It'll be on to the next goal. But for now, I really want it.

Why write this book now? I'm 29 years old and still have a long career ahead of me, but right now, the memories of my earlier races are still so vivid in my mind. I wanted to share what I learned as a 19-year-old on her way to her first international meet, a 20-year-old athlete on the flight to the Olympics less than a year later, and the 28-year-old nursing a difficult injury for a lot of the 2023 season. I wanted to write a book that could inspire and inform young athletes who are just getting started in their journey, because I'm still right there, just a couple of races ahead.

If you ever talk to me in real life—and I hope you will—you'll notice that I say 'thank you' a lot. I like being able to call out moments of gratitude and acknowledge when people say something to me that's really meaningful, or that lifts me up. Part of why I wanted to write this book is that I'm hopeful that something I've been through or something I've learned over my career so far will lift *you* up.

I also wanted to make sure that this book wouldn't just get you thinking, it would make you act as well. So in each chapter, there is a JOURNAL PROMPTS-slash-journalling section with prompts for you to think about. I don't just want to share my story, I want you to think about the stories you want to tell someday!

So, here we are, about to get started. This book is for anyone who's out there chasing their big dreams. Maybe those dreams are on the track, maybe they're in another part of your life. But I don't think anyone who picks up a copy of this book doesn't have a big dream they're going after. Let's go after them together.

-Micha Powell

SPOTLIGHT

PEPSI FLORIDA RELAYS | FLORIDA, USA | 2016

"I did what my conscience told me to do, and you can't fail if you do that."
  —Anita Hill

I can thank my parents for my perseverance because I think if I didn't have parents who understood the struggle, I would have quit this sport a long time ago. It makes a difference when you have people who fundamentally understand the mentality that it takes, the frustrations, and the highs, of being an elite athlete.

But at the same time, it creates a challenge: I felt the need from a young age to create a legacy that would stand as tall as theirs has.

Should you step out of your parents' legacy, or should you step into it?

Having two Olympians as parents sounds pretty great. It sounds like you're destined to be this amazing athlete, to follow in their footsteps. But stepping into someone's track spikes isn't as easy as you'd think. Just because both of my parents are phenoms in the sport doesn't mean that it's any easier to go after big goals. If anything, I have more eyes and more pressure on me. The expectations are higher, and to feel as though I've made it in the sport means thinking about not just matching either parent, but surpassing both. And that comes with its own set of challenges.

If you haven't heard of them—and if you're in track, you probably have—my mother is Rosey Edeh, three-time Olympian and silver medalist in the 400-meter hurdles at the World University Games and world cup gold medalist in the 4x400 relay, and my dad, Mike Powell, is the two-time Olympic silver medalist in the long jump. My mom set the Canadian record for 400-meter hurdles in 1996, and that record stood until 2019. My dad set the long jump world record in 1991 before I was born, and it still stands today. It's the longest-held world record in that sport. Maybe that's why I took so long to find my way to the track—it's a lot to live up to. (That, and my deep love of Serena Williams and her tennis abilities… and her personal style.)

Back in 2013, after years of avoiding it in favor of tennis, I accepted that despite my best efforts, I hung up my racket because I loved the track. I loved running, and I *really* loved the 400 meters. And since I discovered that while still in high school, deciding which colleges to apply to became largely about deciding which track and field program would be best for me. Not something I expected! When I did make my way to the track, and into the 400 meter, I knew I would have to figure out a way to carve my own path, separate from my parents. Luckily, fate seemed to be in my favor.

My journey to deciding to go to the University of Maryland was a bit unconventional. I first applied to three Canadian universities and got accepted to all of them. Initially, that was my plan: I didn't want to follow my mom's footsteps *too* closely. She had gone to school in the US where there was a fuller track experience, where she was able to race in the NCAA. At first, I didn't want that. But as my skills on the track got stronger and more obvious, I started to really think about whether I was avoiding applying to American schools out of fear of failure rather than just because I didn't want to do the same thing as my mom had done.

By the start of senior year, I was training with the club track team at the University of Toronto, taking it much more seriously and thinking about the future. Sure, Canadian schools would be cheaper than American schools—but what if I could get a track scholarship? I wasn't a track phenom like my parents yet. My times were good but not amazing, and the workouts were really challenging, but it felt like it was within my reach. It was just uncomfortable enough training with that club: I was being pushed, I wasn't entirely sure I belonged, but I felt like I was on my way.

With junior track clubs like this one, you do get exposure to universities and recruiters. When the university coaches and recruiters would come to meets, I wasn't nervous—I was so excited. I was not on any recruiter's radar, especially at first. They were actually there to see other girls run. But because I am very loquacious and I love to talk to people, I would go over to chat with them. Being relaxed meant I ran well and I presented myself well, because I wasn't too worried about the impression I would make, I was just being myself. One of those people was Coach Andrew Valmon, who's the head coach at the University of Maryland. He's a former world record holder on the track himself and I didn't know it when I introduced myself, but he knew my parents in the nineties when they were all competing simultaneously. (The track world is quite small!)

Still, my times for the 400 were nothing special for these recruiters, and while he was nice, he wasn't about to recruit me just because he knew my mom and dad. But in my first outdoor season that spring, I started making real progress and dropped my 400-meter time to 56 seconds. And that turned some heads. But it was a race in June at the Ontario Federation of School Association Championships (more commonly referred to as OFSAA and known as the Superbowl of track and field events for Canadian high schoolers), that changed everything. I had already run a 56-second 400, and I felt like I was ready to try for 55 seconds. This doesn't sound like a big jump, but consider that it's an improvement of almost two percent in just a month!

So, I told my club coach at the time that I was going to go out there and run a 55. He said, "No, don't do that." It was my first realization that he had such a limited view of me, that he didn't even want me to try. Here I was, thinking I just wanted to run as fast as I could. That this is so *fun*. For him, he was nervous I wouldn't have enough to finish and would post a bad time.

I chose to ignore him and decided to go for it. At the start line, I was just so excited and so amped because I was about to run against all of the fastest girls in Ontario, and I went from going into that race ranked six to finishing in second, just behind the girl who won... and doing it in 55 seconds. My coach? He was really surprised. Me? I wasn't—and I realized that if I wanted to pursue track, I needed more than a scholarship, I needed a coach who believed in me and was going to encourage me.

Now, improving your time from 59 seconds down to 55 may not sound like a huge deal if you don't race track. But the 400 distance is really hard to progress in, because it's both long and still extremely short. You do have to meter your efforts, you can't just go all out from the gun, sprinting like it's a 100-meter dash. You need to be tactical and have something left in the tank for the final stretch, and it can be hard to know how to pace. But you also have to be going your top speed and there's no room for error. Because of that, there are a lot of different factors at play as you try to drop your times. Just watch someone who's new to that distance in a race against someone who's been doing it for years—you see it really clearly at high school track meets. A longtime athlete is perfecting and crafting the exact execution that's needed. Every tiny thing is being considered, from the way they drive their arms to the way they look ahead. For new runners, dropping one or two seconds from your personal record is normal in your first season as your body learns the distance, but you don't yet understand the tactical side of things, it's all about your speed. Dropping four seconds the way I was able to is not typical. That's the kind of result that coaches start looking at and thinking, 'How can we develop this talent?'

It doesn't stop with talent, but that does get you started.

That 55 seconds didn't just translate to a personal victory, it translated into an offer of a scholarship from Maryland to race and train under Coach Valmon—see? Coaches notice the four second drop down to 55. Getting that invite was obviously enough that it made me go, 'Wow, this is such a huge opportunity.' It also made me want to see if I could get accepted anywhere else, including my mom's alma mater, Rice University, since they had a more established track program than Maryland. They didn't accept me—they just didn't see my time as competitive enough. Racing track in the States is obviously so competitive, so I understood that decision then. (Flash forward two years when I *did* run the Olympic standard, the coach from that program who had initially rejected me from the program ended up apologizing and telling me he should have taken me!)

Things happen for a reason, though, and Maryland was definitely the right choice for me. It didn't have a huge track program but that was a positive for me, since it let me grow and stand out in a lower stress environment. It gave me a closer connection to my coach and my teammates. As someone who was really new to the sport, a big school with a big program likely would have just swallowed me up.

I made the decision to go to Maryland, sight unseen. I never set foot on the campus until a couple of weeks before the first semester started. I just didn't have time with my summer racing schedule. But that didn't worry me: I'm definitely a person who sets my sights on something and just goes for it. Once I make a decision, that's it. I didn't need a tour or orientation to tell me I was going to take the chance on this school, I just felt that it was the right decision.

Luckily, the campus itself was beautiful. That was a nice bonus —it was a great environment where everything I needed was within walking distance. It was close enough to DC to be able to go there when I wanted to be in a city, and the journalism program was amazing. Maryland may not have the warmest climate in the US, but compared to training in Quebec in the winter, training in January in Maryland was no problem at all. (My birthday is in January, and I remember my first winter down there going out to dinner in a lightweight little jacket because it was still 10 degrees

Celsius out.) Back at home in Montreal, we had a couple feet of snow and it was in the negatives. Down here, they would cancel school due to frost! So while everyone around me was complaining about the weather, I was loving it.

Being at Maryland also meant that yes, I was in a new country, but I was only a short flight from home, which meant going home for holidays and having my mom easily fly down for big meets. Even when I was struggling with the idea of being in my mom's shadow as an athlete, I always knew it wasn't about her: she was and is my biggest supporter, and she was always willing to share her experience and knowledge to help me improve.

So there I was, moving away from home and into my dorm, with my mom and grandmother helping me carry my stuff into my new room. I remember holding hands with both of them and they prayed over me before leaving to go back home. They prayed that I would have a wonderful, safe, and joyous experience on this campus. I'll never forget that.

And it was a wonderful experience, though it definitely wasn't always joyous or smooth. Workouts were hard, classes were harder, and learning to get along in a team environment when you're still sort of new to the sport is always going to be a challenge. On university teams, the stakes are higher than they ever were in high school, and looking back, it's easy to see how as young adults, we formed little cliques within the team and social dynamics played a key role in team dynamics. As an only child, being part of a close-knit team took some getting used to.

My mom had warned me that it would be an adjustment, getting used to the tight team environment. She was right. I would call her to tell her I'd had an argument or disagreement with one of the girls on the team at practice, and I'd be so upset. I took every-thing personally, especially in those first couple of months, because I didn't know how else to take things! Even the smallest disagree-ment would affect me.

It took a long time to realize that instead of being upset about these moments of friction, I needed to stand up for myself, even for the little things. And the moment I did, I realized how much time

I'd wasted being upset instead of confronting situations head on. It took years: I remember even my junior year, I was still dealing with the desire to fit in rather than stand up for myself. That January, we were having a team dinner the same day as my birthday and I had asked the coach if I could invite a couple of friends to join us. He said it was fine, but apparently, some of my teammates weren't happy about that. Instead of telling me that they had an issue with it, one of them was talking about it at dinner on the other end of the table. He accused me of being a bad teammate, a bad team captain. I didn't hear about it until the next day when a friend told me what had been said. I was devastated. I called my coach crying. I told him the situation, and the first thing he said was, "You need to stand up for yourself, no one else can do that for you. But you can't confront him emotionally. You have to be the team leader." He also reminded me that my goal was running, and that if it's what I wanted to do, I'd have to be able to not let external things get in the way. I would need a tougher skin if I wanted to be a pro athlete.

He was right. I was a complete mess and I wouldn't be able to confront that teammate from a calm place. So, once I calmed down, I talked to him. He hid behind another guy and blamed someone else. He was terrified of me once I stepped into that space of being able to stand up for myself. That experience obviously is one that I look back at and laugh at now—it was such a silly little thing. But at the time, it was such a big deal in my world. The other big deal in my world, the one Coach Valmon was telling me to focus on above all else, was excelling on the track team, and securing a school record. I'm not sure why it mattered to me so much, but I instinctively knew that getting a school record would make me feel like I was starting to build my own legacy.

Once I got to Maryland, I was training with people who were better than me. And then I slowly started to get better as a result— that's probably the biggest secret to success and the hardest one to get used to. Being the best doesn't mean that you're the fastest one in your training group, especially when you first get started. You make gains not by being the best runner in your group, but by having faster runners to emulate and to chase. For those four years in university, I was always pushed. There was one girl on the team who used to butt heads with me, but not in a negative way. We pushed each other to be better because we were competitive with each other, and I'm so thankful for her. That's hard to find outside of the high school and collegiate athletic systems, but it's something that all runners should be looking for.

I had a good start freshman year, but nothing groundbreaking. Part of me was a little disappointed to not instantly be a huge success at this school, but I could see progress. I got down to 53 seconds in the 400 meter. I was one spot away from making it to Regionals that year, which represents a big milestone as a collegiate runner. Also, I was only two seconds away from the school record (which yes, is a huge amount of time on the track, but still!).

Sophomore year, my coach and I sat down in his office, and I circled every record in the school book that I wanted to break. That list turned it into a game, and also a reality. More importantly, this was also the moment where I chose to step out of my dad's shadow. That day, looking at the school records, we came to the long jump. My dad, as I've said, still holds the long jump world record. At that point, he wasn't in my life, but with his name and by racing on the track, people knew we were connected and there was this expectation that I would grow into the long jump. It just made sense. But my coach, who knew my dad, looked at me in that moment and said, "I think you should carve your own path. And it should be 'Micha Powell runs the 400.' Not 'Mike Powell's daughter does the long jump.'" The long jump may have been the easier route. But I needed to carve out my own identity.

Neither of my parents put any kind of pressure or expectations on me to follow in their footsteps. I knew they both wanted me to reach my best, but they weren't pushing me to make as many Olympic teams or bring home as many medals as they had. I was the one putting that pressure on myself, and at the time, there was part of me that wondered if they weren't putting the pressure on me because they didn't really believe in me.

I was really starting to settle into my own lane as a runner and as a team leader, and my breakthrough finally came my junior year.

I broke the indoor *and* outdoor 400 meter record for the school. Talk about momentum. The outdoor record came after I went to NCAA East Indoors for the first time in 2016, and it was a tight turnaround to the start of the outdoor season. It felt strange, making that indoor to outdoor track shift within a week—the surfaces and styles of racing are actually a lot different. I'd had a good indoor season, but still, getting into outdoor mode just feels weird, even if you're feeling good. It was just one thing after another, but at the time, that fast pace felt good for me.

The first outdoor race of the season was down in Florida, and it was a hot day—again, different from indoor where everything is really dialed, including the temperature. I was doing my warmup and taking my time, just feeling pretty relaxed. I walked over to where we'd be corralled before getting onto the track for our race feeling confident and calm... only to realize that I'd left my track spikes on the other side of the stadium. The second I realized it, my heart sank and I bolted back to grab them. I got back with just enough time to very quickly pull them on and lace up, all while trying to stay calm but internally freaking out. I had less than a minute to get ready for this race, I could feel the adrenaline pumping through my body, and I was trying to stay as steady as possible as I made my way to the blocks with absolutely no time to spare.

I barely remember being in the blocks, I just remember the gun going off and then I was up and running. I was in the second heat of the day in a very competitive field. Almost immediately, the girl who started just behind me on the track—who had beat me at indoor championships just a week earlier—ran past me. I knew that was a bad sign, but I was starting to get back into the groove after that initial adrenaline spike before the start.

I thought to myself, 'She's fast, but I think I can keep up. I can use this.' I marked her and focused on reeling her in. In the last 50 meters, I came past her, finishing as strong as I ever have. I could barely see after crossing the line I was so out of energy but I could hear them announce the times and mine was a 52.4. The girl I passed was patting me on the back and congratulating me, and I could hear my coach cheering. I just remember thinking how weird it was that less than two minutes earlier, everyone was yelling at me to hurry up and berating me for forgetting my spikes.

And then my coach told me that I had broken the school record, which had stood for 17 years. It was one of those moments where you couldn't have planned it. I wouldn't have guessed that that race was going to be when I broke the school record outdoors. Everything wasn't perfectly set up. Everything didn't go according to plan. But I saw the chance to go for it and I did.

Breaking the school record, I felt closer to my mom and my dad because I knew they had so many records themselves. It marked the first big break in my own career, and while it felt like I was closer to them, in another way, it felt like it was the first time that I stepped out of their long shadows and into my own spotlight.

I think deep inside, I knew that if I could stop feeling as though I was standing in their shadows, I would be able to find that sense of personal belonging, see my truth, and finally believe in myself as *me*, not as their daughter.

Once I got into my 400 meter groove, there was no turning back. I was all in, just focusing on that distance. I had initially circled a few other school records that I wanted to achieve, but I realized that a scattered approach wouldn't achieve much. I might get a few more school records, sure, but I wouldn't go far beyond that. I needed to hone my craft, and my superpower was the 400 meter.

I was standing on my own feet—or in my own track spikes. I would do a different event than either of my parents. I was at a different school. I could be my own athlete. I would create my own legacy, my way. Yes, there would be parallels to my parents. My mom still holds her school record, my dad still has the world record. But while I was following in their footsteps, I was still carving out my own part of the path.

But it wasn't going to be a straightforward one. I quickly realized that the faster you get, the harder it is to drop your times. It's a math thing: the lower you go, the greater the percentage of change for even the slightest improvement in your time. So you often see big jumps early in your career, and then it stabilizes and you have to fight for every hundredth of a second, or even to continue getting the times you got once. Breakthroughs are a blessing and a curse: You break a record once, and you assume it'll be easy to do that again. But it's not.

And now, I was in the spotlight.

SPRINT THROUGH YOUR SETBACKS JOURNAL PROMPTS

Grab a notebook or just jot your ideas down on these pages!

WHAT LEGACY (OR LEGACIES) DO YOU WANT TO LEAVE BEHIND?

So much of my story is about the desire to create legacies for myself, and I think that's something everyone wants! Think about this in a few ways: Try 1 year, 5 years and then, your whole life legacy. This helps bring it a little bit closer to the present day and feel more achievable rather than some esoteric exercise you'll do once and forget about!

My 1 year legacy will be...
(Example: setting the school record)
Ways you're working towards this:
1.
2.
3.

My 5 year legacy will be...
(Example: going to the Olympics)
Ways you're working towards this:
1.
2.
3.

My lifelong legacy will be...
(Example: being known as a runner who gave back)
Ways you're working towards this:
1.
2.
3.

SETTING YOURSELF UP FOR SUCCESS

My story towards that school record really began the day I was at the track in Toronto and introduced myself to the coach from the University of Maryland. If I hadn't gone up and said hello and started a conversation, maybe he would have noticed my running ability, but he may not have been as interested in bringing me onto the team. Whenever I'm in a new situation, I try to introduce myself to the people around me and have real conversations, because you never know what could come from that. (That's actually how this book came about!) It's such a superpower to think, 'Okay, how am I going to take up space in this room? How am I going to put myself in the best possible situation?' This is true for athletics, it's true for friendships and relationships, it's true for school and work. Even if you're a naturally shy person, you can still show up and own a room.

Your journal exercise:

- Write a list of people you'd love to interact with more than you currently do. How can you start more meaningful conversations with them?
- What are some conversation starters that you can remember for when you do meet new people?
- Is there a mantra or even something you can do physically to get yourself in the 'I got this' mindset when meeting new people? (These can be cues like standing up straight, counting to five in your head and then saying hello, or just telling yourself 'I've got this.')

CAN YOU USE COMPARISON OR ENVY AS A MOTIVATOR?

A big part of my story is comparing myself to both of my parents, but everyone has people they compare themselves to or envy. Maybe there's someone on social media who you constantly compare yourself to or maybe it's someone in your class. Comparison and envy can be bad, if you let them turn your thinking negative. But you can also use them as information and motivation. I've always tried to see my parents' successes as motivators for my own.

Your journal exercise:

- Make a list of a few people you often compare yourself to or who's life you wish you had.
- From that list, write down what it is about those people that makes you compare yourself to them. What do you wish you had that they have? (Sometimes making this list actually shows you that you don't really want their life, you just like how it looks on Instagram... but sometimes it actually helps you see what goals really matter to you!)
- Now that you know what exactly you're envious of or comparing yourself to, you can make a plan to work towards achieving that goal for yourself!

BEGINNER

"I've learned that people will forget what you said, people will forget what you did, but people will never forget how you made them feel."
—Maya Angelou

Racing for your high school, your local club team, or your university is one thing, but racing for your *country* at an international level is something completely different. I think no matter how long you've been doing local track races, nothing entirely prepares you for stepping up to that next level, with all of the new dynamics and pieces of the puzzle that go with it.

Despite having earned a scholarship to run at the University of Maryland, being a collegiate athlete, and having some early local success, when I got on the plane for my first race with the Canadian National Team in Costa Rica in August of 2015, I was out of my comfort zone. I felt like I'd never done a race before in my life—at least, not like this, not on an international stage. I was suddenly a complete beginner, almost in a way that I'd never felt before because the stakes felt much higher than they ever had been. There were so many unknowns for me: I was gearing up for my third year at university, packing to move back to Maryland, and here I was, getting on a plane.

But I was still thrilled when I got the email selecting me to be on this team. The excitement outweighed the nerves by a mile, and when I first got my national team kit that I would be running in, I stood in front of the mirror wearing it, seeing myself as an athlete who would be representing not just her club or school, but for the first time, her nation. I remember taking a selfie in it—back when it was still with my digital camera, not with my phone.

That kit was special because 2015 was the last year of that design (in every Olympic cycle, they change the gear for the next four years). It felt special that my first team kit was the last time that kit would be used. It was the same outfit design that the 2012 Olympic team wore, which was the Olympic team that made me want to run. Back in 2012, I told my mom that I had decided I wanted to go to the Olympics—and I think part of it was because of how much I loved that year's kit since it reminded me of the one that my mom wore in the 1996 Atlanta Olympic Games. I could imagine myself sporting the bold red singlet with CANADA emblazoned across the chest as I sprinted through the finish line!

Planning out what I was going to bring for this trip, I definitely packed way too much. No one else brought as many suitcases as me! I just didn't want to be underprepared. I wanted to show up and show the coaches that I was entirely ready to go, a total professional already.

On the flight, I started to debate how I was supposed to be feeling and acting around my new teammates. Should I play it cool? Could I share how excited I am? Should I be this super serious, focused racer or should I try to make friends? Personally, I was finally feeling like I was earning my stripes in the sport, like I was really an elite athlete.

This 2015 track season was the year before the Rio Olympics, which meant the nerves and the stakes weren't too intense… at least, at that particular moment. Making my first National Team the year before the Olympics meant I had the opportunity to experience what it would be like representing my country, without the undeniable pressure of performing at a Games. The team I made was racing at the North American, Central American and Caribbean WACAC 2015 Senior Championships. I was still new to the sport: I'd only been racing for two years competitively, so I was still learning a lot about running the 400 meter race and I was not focusing on results at World Championships in Beijing that year or the upcoming Olympics just yet. I was thinking about starting the next semester of university in a month and hopefully being named team captain. I was also officially starting my journalism program in the fall and couldn't wait to be an upperclassman.

Planning a track and field season can be confusing even for those of us who race regularly, especially in the beginning, and even more so when you're trying to follow along with both university-level track racing and elite track racing. In this case, for the Canadian track and field season, racing at NACAC wasn't such a big deal because we were bringing a team of people who hadn't made the Worlds team. In fact, even those of us on the team referred to ourselves as the B team! I didn't mind—I was just excited to be brought on for any race.

I also knew I had a lot to learn about international racing, so having the pressure around the race be a bit lower was helpful since I was already so excited and nervous regardless. International competitions are logistically demanding for athletes: We're often trying to figure out things like the competition schedule and rules and check-ins in another language—in this case, Spanish.

I'd never been to Costa Rica before, and I remember the coaches kept stressing how dangerous it was going to be where we were and how we weren't going to be able to see much outside of our hotel and the track. So my image of it being a fun trip with plenty of chances for tourism definitely got squashed early on—which was very good practice for the rest of my career, since a lot of international races don't leave much time for travel and sightseeing. Basically, when you're at an event like this, you go from the hotel to the track and back again. Most of your meals? At the hotel. Team meetings? At the track, or at the hotel. If you're lucky, you have a bit of time to check out the streets right near the hotel, but there's never tourism on the agenda. You're there for work. Glamorous? Not really.

Our plane bumped down into the small airport near San Jose and looking out the window, I saw that we were surrounded by mountains and lush, green trees. It looked like a movie set, not real life. At this particular meet, at least our hotel in San Jose has everything included. There was a gorgeous outdoor blue pool. (Admittedly, none of us went swimming because we soon found out that during this time of year, it didn't go much higher than 20 degrees Celsius in Costa Rica—not warm enough for a swim in a freezing pool.)

The hotel itself was huge and my teammates and had so much fun knocking on each others doors, exploring the many halls of building and going for short errands at the nearby grocery market. (That was about all we could do, since we couldn't go anywhere else without supervision at the risk of being kidnapped. I think they were being a bit dramatic!) Nevertheless, we made the most of being isolated at the meet hotel.

The team was mostly beginners like myself, but there were a few runners who had been on national teams before—and a couple of them didn't seem thrilled to be on this B team with us newbies. This happens frequently in elite sports with national teams: there are older athletes who are close to making the big teams for races like Worlds but don't quite make the cut that season. They're still good, they're still racing well, so they get brought on smaller trips like this, where they're expected to race well but also be mentors and role models for the newer athletes. Unfortunately, not every athlete sees that as a privilege, and not every athlete views the opportunity to serve as a mentor as a positive thing. On this team, I remember one girl in particular was not excited about being one of the older runners in our crew. She was snapping at everyone, both the athletes and the coaches.

Luckily, she was in the minority, and everyone else was really happy to be there, so there was this nervous but positive energy from the minute we got off the plane. We were all just buzzing...

possibly because being stuck between just the track and hotel meant we all had a lot of extra energy to burn. We'd go to the track, do a little workout, come back to our rooms. This is before streaming shows on Netflix was really a thing, so there was a lot of downtime and not a lot to do to fill it.

Finally, the first day of the meet came. And this is where my very young, inexperienced self was completely thrown off by how different everything was. As I signed in, I realized that none of the volunteers spoke English, and none of the signs or information was in English. Luckily, one of the girls in our race heat spoke enough English that she was able to help us, and we're so lucky that she did. Looking back, she didn't have to do that, she could have just let us flounder. It was kind of her and I'll never forget that.

The nerves of not understanding the language may have actually helped me: they squashed all of the nerves I had about the race itself, and instead, I was fully focused on just trying to figure out how to navigate the start line and the rules and what the announcers were saying!

Our new friend was translating for the volunteers, telling us how the race was going to go. I admit, I thought that was a little strange, because I did think that there was a chance she could just be telling us the wrong thing on purpose to mess us up. But I decided to trust her and assume the best. It got weirder from that point and as we all went to our blocks, there was something going on with the announcers' microphones, so we really couldn't hear them at all. When they did get everything working—sort of—I realized that didn't help us much, since the instructions they were announcing were still all in Spanish. "Ready, set, go?" Nope, it was "en sus marcas, listos, ¡ya!" and we were off, slightly confused but running our race.

Just a few seconds into the race, though, I thought I heard something in Spanish from the announcer over the loudspeaker, and the girl next to me—our translator!—started to slow down. So I start thinking, 'Oh, no, did they call us back? What's happening?' while I'm still running.

And here is the key advice from this chapter. If you take one thing away from this entire book, remember this: *do not stop*. Do not stop, no matter what. You keep going until it's absolutely clear that the race is called. Someone should basically be tackling you off the track to get you to stop.

The worst case if you keep running after they've called the race is that you'll do an extra portion of a lap and someone will step out in front of you to stop you if they really did call it. But in something like the 400 where milliseconds count, you can't slow down to try to listen to what the announcer is saying. You get distracted by another runner and your race is over.

Run your own race. Do not stop.

But no, I made the rookie mistake. I didn't entirely stop, but I slowed down so much that I was able to look around and realize, 'Oh, the race is still going.'

I absolutely butchered my first race on an international scale, on an international stage.

It was a lesson I needed to learn, and I never repeated that mistake. It was a reminder to stay in your own lane—track pun obviously intended—and stay focused on *you*. I still have no idea why that girl slowed down. Maybe her leg was cramped, maybe she heard the same thing as me and panicked. But I shouldn't have let her slowdown impact me.

I crossed the line in last, but my racing in Costa Rica thankfully didn't end there. I had a bad race, but I was still going to be on the relay because I was still one of the strongest girls running the four by four, which is the four-hundred meter relay with four runners.

I had a bad race, but I wasn't a bad runner... at least, that's what I told myself. On the bus back to the hotel, the older girl on the team sat down next to me and I thought she'd give me some advice, maybe tell me a story about a time she had a bad race, something like that. Nope. She leans over and says, "Don't mess the relay up."

I just sat there in a bit of shock. I get it: I had a bad race, I lost focus, I messed up my 400 meter run. But heading into the relay, that wasn't the advice I was looking for. It was just so unnecessary, but I didn't have the confidence to say that to her. I was just taken aback.

When you run the individual 400 meter, it's pretty much a given that you also run in the four by four relay. It's the expectation. I love the individual 400 meter, but the four by four is special because each one of you knows the pain of running a quarter mile. I think it's actually the most fun of the events because you get to feed off each other, and the energy is sort of transferred from runner to runner each time you pass the baton. It's invigorating to have your teammates counting on you.

Luckily, when it came time for the four by four, I didn't mess up. I went in and did my job. I held my own as the youngest one on the team. In the race, we didn't podium, but we did make up a lot of ground on the teams in front of us. We improved on the expectations for our team, so it may not have been a dramatic win, but it was a good moment and the coaches were happy with the performance, which was good for me given how my first race had gone. So it definitely was a good send-off. (And it's no surprise that the girl who told me 'not to mess it up' left the sport soon after.)

I realized on that trip that it was possible to have one bad race, and not let it ruin the rest of the event. There's always another chance. And what came out of that first international meet was being able to laugh at myself. That's an embarrassing moment, basically stopping in the middle of a race that's less than a minute long. It was like one of those nightmares you have where you're watching yourself doing something that's so embarrassing and in the dream, you just want to yell at yourself to stop. But one awkward moment like that doesn't define you, it just teaches you to grow from it. Now that I'm 10 years into the sport, nothing can really faze me because I know I have a job to do and I have enough experience under my belt to rely on if I find myself in an intimidating situation.

The other thing that trip taught me was about the kind of leader I wanted to be. That girl who told me not to mess up had an opportunity on that trip to stand up and be the team leader and really help the younger athletes, but she didn't take advantage of that. I have no idea what was going on in her life that made her act like that, but I remember how she made me feel.

When I'm in those situations with younger athletes now, whether or not I'm the oldest athlete or the one who is supposed to be leading, I choose love and I work to create a good environment for everyone. Ultimately, she actually taught me how I want to treat other young athletes. If I hadn't had that experience with her, maybe I wouldn't have thought about how I act with new runners. And it doesn't take much: switch "don't mess it up" to "you've got this." Same number of words, entirely different vibe. I've been told by head coaches that one of my biggest assets on the relay is that they can always count on me to be a team player.

Sometimes, that can obviously be a little bit to my detriment and I know that I have to find that balance of speaking up for myself and not being everyone's mom while still being a good leader, but I'll always try to make the team the best they can be. There is a fine line when being too much of that 'helpful teammate' can mean that you're the one who gives all of their energy to others, leaving nothing left for yourself. Being a good teammate means being supportive, but it doesn't mean being supportive *at the cost of your result*. We often see girls and women in news stories being praised for stopping in their race to help a teammate or competitor, but while that's a great headline, I do think that's just maintaining this narrative that as women, we have to be nurturers rather than competitors. I see those stories and think, "Oh, that's a nice moment, but that athlete just lost the chance to win a race or have a great day." There's a fine line to walk between being a supportive teammate and being a good competitor. You can give a teammate encouragement and have a moment together before the race. But when the starter pistol goes off, you need to be 100 percent focused on the job at hand, which is running as fast as you can, not paying attention to everything around you.

That may sound callous, but on the track, remember, there are medical professionals, volunteers and coaches there. Me stopping my race because someone else tripped doesn't help any of us. And flipping it, if I fell on the track, I wouldn't want someone else to ruin their race to help me. I don't want that guilt. The race is not the time for a Hallmark movie moment. If you want to be a great track racer, you have to have the "I'm going to win this race" mentality and you can't be sidetracked watching what's going on around you. This is your career on the line.

I want to be known as a supportive, friendly teammate, but also as a fierce competitor. You have to be able to switch between the two. Just two years into the sport, and I was learning one of the biggest lessons I would learn: with every interaction, you're creating a legacy. Whether it's in a race or on the team bus, everything you do is one step closer to how you'll be remembered.

Grab a notebook or just jot your ideas down on these pages!

MOVE THROUGH EMBARRASSING MOMENTS WITH GRACE—AND GET SMARTER ALONG THE WAY!

What's one embarrassing moment that you can reframe into a lesson?

Looking back at that embarrassing moment (since we're there anyway!)... Does it matter at all now? Did it change your life? If you asked people who were there about it, would anyone even remember? We often build these moments up in our minds as huge life moments, but if you get honest about it, you often realize that it wasn't as bad as you thought.

What about a tiny embarrassing moment you've had or a little mistake you made recently? How can you grow from that small moment? (Growth doesn't just happen with big things!)

CREATE A 'LET IT GO' RITUAL

The next time an embarrassing moment happens (and it will!) or you make a mistake, what's a little ritual or routine that you can do to move past it? Maybe it's a certain song, maybe you vow to take five minutes to journal on it in your Notes app, maybe you just plan to text a good friend with a certain emoji so they know to say something nice. Having this ready will make the next not-so-great moment much easier to move through.

DECIDE NOW HOW YOU WANT TO BE KNOWN

You create a legacy not just in your actions, but in how you make other people feel when they're around you. You've already decided on your legacy in the Spotlight chapter, but now, get clear on how you want people to really remember you.

- What impact do you want to have on people? How do you want people to feel after aninteraction with you?
- How would you like to be described by someone who knows you? (This can be a sentence or just a few words that you hope would describe you.)
- Go beyond that... what do you want to be known for in terms of achieving your goals? (This can be things like 'she always gets things done on time' or 'she's a fierce competitor.' These may not be the first things that come to mind for how you want to be described as a person—this is about your goal achievement and work ethic!)
- Bonus points: actually bring a friend or two into this exercise and ask them to write down a few words or sentences that describe you, and do the same for them. Check what they said versus how you want to be seen. If the two don't match, that's not a bad thing—it's just something to think about! (For example, in high school I definitely would have said that I was someone who always did her own thing, but looking back, I bet my friends actually would have described me as someone who got along with everyone and worked hard to fit in! That information would have been great, because it would have reminded me to be more of an individual and to be proud of that.)
- Sum it up: what are the 3-5 words you want to describe yourself with, after doing those exercises? Are there ways you can lean into those words a little more?

CALM

"When I dare to be powerful — to use my strength in the service of my vision, then it becomes less and less important whether I am afraid."
  –Audre Lorde

Junior year of university, as Regionals rolled around, I was ready to make the team. A track season is a big chain of cause and effect because most of it is doing well enough at competitions to be invited to or qualify for the next competition. When it comes to the collegiate NCAA Nationals, they only take top 12 athletes from each region, East and West. So at Regionals, I needed to run a top 12. But first, I needed to get there.

Basically, in collegiate track, not only does every race count, every race determines what the next race is that you can do. That means every race matters as much as Nationals, in a way. If you don't perform well enough to qualify for Regionals, you don't have the chance to even try to compete to go to Nationals. So the first hurdle was qualifying for Regionals at Conference Championships, where it gets decided who's going to Regionals.

It's not just logistically difficult, it's also really hard to periodize to peak for all of the races at which you need to perform. A race like Conference Championships isn't as important as Nationals, obviously… until you realize that if you don't race your best there, you won't have the chance to show up at Regionals in order to race to compete at Nationals! So in a way, it's actually a *more* important race.

At Conference Championships, also known as the Big Ten Championships, I was going in as the favorite to at least come top three, and I was feeling very fast and very confident. The race was in a small town near Lincoln, Nebraska, and there, all of the work I'd been putting in for the last three years felt like it finally fell into place.

Ideally, I had wanted to win the Conference Championships for my team. I made it to the finals for the 400 meter with no problems, and my coach told me, "Don't be afraid to go for it." I took that to heart. I don't think I've ever started as fast as I did in that race. I suffered so much in that minute, and unfortunately, that was only good enough for fourth. I was going to Regionals, but I didn't hit the mark I had hoped to to hit for my team that day.

We still had the 400-meter relay that weekend at Conference Championships, so I gave myself a pretty stern talking to about needing to regroup and get back in the game. I was running anchor, meaning I was the last person to run, and by the time it was my turn to go, we were sitting in last place. I had a few seconds to set my mindset as I waited for the baton: I could stay in this defeated feeling from my race and just accept us being in last, or I could do everything I could to move us up. As I took the baton from my teammate in last place, I channeled that disappointment with my earlier performance into something good. I reminded myself that I *can* run fast, I *can* execute on a plan. I used every person in front of me as a chess piece, catching one person after another, eventually moving us all the way from last to winning our heat.

Regionals were waiting. I was ready.

But going into Regionals wasn't the end goal. I needed to have a good race there in order to make it to Nationals, which were happening the next month in Portland, Oregon. Confusing, I know. We needed flowcharts and spreadsheets just to figure out what races I needed to do in order to race again!

So, getting on that flight to Florida for the race, I knew there was a lot at stake.

My warmup was really intentional for the first round of racing at Regionals, which determines if you were going to make it into the Quarterfinals. And Quarterfinals are where it's determined if you're going to Nationals or not. Again, confusing. It's just one race after another. (A good rule to live by is just racing every race like you need a good result to move on, since in most of them, that's the case!)

I mostly knew who my competitors were, I'd raced with them in our conference or seen them at Regionals in past years, and of course, in our sport, you follow along with other runner's best times. So I knew I would need to run well to get into Quarterfinals, but I was relatively confident that I'd make it.

I ran smooth and hit a low 52, good enough to get into the Quarterfinals, but was ranked 16th. To get to Nationals means being in the top 12, so 16th meant it wasn't impossible, but that I'd have to bring my A game if I was going to make it.

So, I was going to bring my A game. Easy. Sort of.

Jacksonville's track where Regionals were being held is notorious for spotty weather. One second it's sunny, then the clouds roll in. And the storms bring this heavy feeling to the air. It's more than just humidity, it feels like you're being weighed down. As I got ready to warm up, it was clear that there was a storm just trying to break through.

Then, when I was warming up on the track, the clouds just opened up and all of us sprinted for shelter as it started pouring. It rained just long enough that I started to question whether or not I should just finish my warm up out there in the rain when it stopped. The air was still heavy, and thunder was rumbling a bit, but now that the rain passed, I felt this sense of energy and electricity rather than foreboding.

I actually felt really energized rather than stressed about being thrown off of my rhythm because of that change of pace. With track, everything can feel so regimented that sometimes, a break from the norm is actually the best thing for you. I was doing my last few strides and feeling so good. My coach could see that I was flying. He told me to do just one more stride, and do it strong.

In the past, I'd noticed my best races happened when I was at my most calm. I'm not tired or lacking energy, I just have this calm focus that comes over me. I feel in tune with my body. And I think my coach, at that moment, knew that I was right there.

I did my last stride strong.

Then, I gave Coach a nod, grabbed my things, and headed to the holding area. When you're in races like this, you have to get checked in pretty close to the race start so that they know you're there and you can get your lane assignment. Usually, about 20 minutes before the race is the ideal time to do that. With the rain impacting my warmup, I knew I was close but I had a few minutes before I'd be too late and I wasn't feeling rushed or stressed about it.

I walked up to the check in, and the woman at the desk said, "You're Micha, right?" and I said yes, thinking she knew all the athletes who were there by how we looked. But then, she said, "Do you know how I know it's you?" I shook my head. Then, she said, "It's because you're last."

I couldn't believe what she said. In hindsight, I know she didn't mean it like I was destined to finish last or something, but in that moment, it felt like it. I was like, 'Oh, my gosh, why would you say that to someone?' I was already thinking about how I needed to be top 12, and heading into the Quarterfinals, I was ranked 16th. So I *really* didn't want to hear that.

I shook it off as best I could, trying to not let "you're last" start circling around in my brain. I didn't want to let any negative energy in. As I walked out into the stadium, there was real electricity in the air. The ground was wet, but the air felt lighter and that energy was still pumping. Rather than feeling like the weather was working against me, I felt like it focused me. I really felt like I was where I was meant to be. My coach looked at me, and he's so calm and so sure of me. He just says, "You've got this." It was the exact opposite experience from my coach who told me *not* to go for 55 seconds all those years ago. This time, my coach's energy, his attitude, his belief, were exactly what I needed. I told him, "I'm going to fight."

My race was the second of the Quarterfinal heats, which already felt lucky: it's my favorite to run, because you've seen the times for the first heat, so you have a better sense of what you need to run in order to advance. You also see how the race officials are: are they calling everyone to the line really quickly or is it a little slower pace? Having that information ahead of your heat may not seem like it would make a difference, but anything you can know ahead of time to be more prepared helps you stay calmer on the start line. The second heat is also ideal because you're not in the last heat, so you don't have quite as much time to be nervous. It's just right: a little information so you're more prepared, but not so much time that you're sitting around getting stressed.

I don't ever watch the entire race in the heat ahead of me, since I want to be in my own focused, calm state, but I do watch the start and I'm usually aware of the race as it finishes. I try not to look at the runners themselves and just focus on the information and their times. In this first heat, one of the highest-ranked runners in the conference ran a 50.7, and I remember thinking 'that's fast, but I can get into that range.' I'd never run under 52 at that point, but that day, it felt possible.

I stepped up to the line. I was in lane eight with just one other lane outside of me where there would be a girl I could chase. If you've never watched a track race, it's a weird thing: the lanes are staggered since the distance in the inside lane is shorter around the track than the outside lane by a few meters. That means you're not running side by side with the other runners, you're staggered by several meters at the start. Usually, being in the middle lane is preferable since you're chasing people *and* being chased by other runners. People who are in the middle lanes kind of get to be in the race more, because they get to feel it develop. They also know when to speed up a bit or when they can keep their pace because they're within striking distance of someone, and can even use the feeling of someone behind them to stay motivated. Lanes 1 and 9 are the least ideal to be in, since you're either chasing or being chased. Lane 8 isn't much better: I'd have to rely on myself to push, because I wouldn't be able to see where anyone else was unless they were passing me—and I didn't want that. I took a deep breath and I got in my blocks. The stadium went quiet, but the energy remained. 'Let me just focus on executing,' I thought to myself as I put my hands down to the ground and looked ahead, down the track.

The gun sounded, and I just started running. I could hear my steps, I could feel how hard I was moving. I could actually hear the consistent cadence of my feet going as they hit the damp track. I could hear my heart beating. I've never felt so aware yet so in the zone in a race before.

Within seconds of starting, I'd picked off the girl in Lane 9. That meant I was out front, but I had no idea what was happening behind me. All I knew was that now, I was at least in eighth place. But passing her gave me a second surge of momentum and I was running all out, like someone was chasing me. Which, of course, they were.

By the 200 meter mark, I realized I still couldn't see or feel anyone right behind me. I was running the best race of my life, and I could feel that ticket to Nationals right there in front of me. I felt like the win was possible.

As I ran down the next straightaway, I started to feel my legs cramping as the lactic acid flooded them. I was running out of steam. And at the very edge of my peripheral vision, I saw a girl coming up alongside me. I couldn't tell if everyone else was coming up behind her or if she was out front as well, but seeing her gave me the extra bit of energy I needed to keep pushing.

My mom had preemptively bought a ticket to Oregon when I made it into Regionals. As I hit the final straightaway with the girl at my heels, I just remember thinking, 'My mom didn't buy her ticket to Oregon to come to Nationals for no reason.' She put it out into the universe that I was going to make it to Nationals.

All of this is happening in my head while I'm running. I don't know how I had the energy to think that thought, or why that was what went through my mind instead of something simpler, like 'fast' or 'go!' But that's what I thought of. I was fully focused on the moment, but at the same time, there was part of my brain that was almost cheerleading me by providing a logical reason to keep enduring.

That last 100 meters is torture if you're doing it right. Your muscles have used up all of the oxygen available to them, and yet, you're asking them for more. They're screaming at you. You feel like you're about to die. You don't know where you are in the race, because we're staggered on the start, so you can't even feel secure in your position, you just know you need to push as hard as you possibly can. It's not a person, it's just pure will that crosses the finish line.

To this day, I remember running and thinking about my mom and her *airfare*. It makes no sense. But it's a feeling I keep chasing in races now, because it works: there's the perfect balance of being relaxed enough to have those kinds of thoughts, but also focused enough to keep pushing. And I did keep pushing: I came second in my heat, third overall, and was so close to winning. The girl behind me got me in the end, but by the tiniest margin—and that barely mattered, because her pushing me is probably the reason I was able to run under 52. I ran a 51.97.

My coach was beaming. He was so excited for me. I didn't realize what I did in that moment, but it was a new school record, beating my previous record from that season, plus it took me from 16th in the standings up to fourth—cementing my trip to Nationals.

I was so proud of myself because I not only ran a personal best, not only beat my own school record, but ran below the Olympic standard of 52.20 by .23 seconds. To this day, that run at Regionals is my personal best in the 400. It happened not just because I believed in me, but because in that moment, others believed in my ability. I could feel that energy from my coach, and at that point in my journey, I needed someone who thought I could perform to that ability. I had him in my corner, and my mom was coming to watch me race Nationals.

When you prepare for the race, you focus on your execution, and having these reminders of why you're doing the thing—for me, the fact that my mom had already bought her plane ticket to Nationals—it's the perfect combination.

What people don't tell you about these moments, though, is the honest truth: that they hurt. Yes, it was so great for me to walk off the track knowing that I gave it my all. But I was in so much pain afterwards! I'll paint you a picture: You just cross the finish line, you're thrilled with your performance, but you feel worse than you've ever felt with the flu, with mono, with any kind of illness. It feels like your gums are bleeding. Every time you take a breath, something aches. Your legs feel heavy, like you can't take another step. You've run out of usable oxygen, and your muscles are screaming at you to just stop. It's taking everything you have just to stay standing, but you're still trying to smile for the cameras. It's terrible. Every part of me, from my hairline to my fingertips and every muscle in my legs, just wants to lay down on the ground and stop moving.

Still, that day I walked off the track as smoothly as I could, because my coach always told us that after a race, you walk away looking strong because you don't want your opponents to see you on the ground. That's just part of being a competitor: you want to leave your best self out there and keep walking even if it hurts.

I was also on cloud nine, despite the pain. There's a feeling of euphoria when you finish running your fastest time, and it's even more so when you did it at a meet that counted. It's unreal. It doesn't matter how sore you feel.

But then, there's the aftermath. The trickiest part of track is always the team element: you're a team, but at the same time, you're racing as individuals and that can be a little hard to navigate at meets. You have the best race of your career, but someone else on your team probably had their worst run. In our team's case, this was even more obvious because we're a small team, so it's really clear who's had a good day and who hasn't. The bigger schools don't have this problem as much, because the teams are so big that if one person had a bad day, it's not a big deal. At a race like this, where you're finding out if you're going to Nationals, it's even more apparent how small our team is compared to the big schools. So I think I held back some of my own excitement because I was aware that some of my teammates hadn't made it. It's always hard to know if you should have taken the moment to really celebrate and get excited, but I think looking back and knowing you were a gracious teammate is better than having had the full celebration.

That 51-second result led to me to not just the NCAA Nationals, but to my first Olympic team. It was also the point where suddenly, a lot of comparisons were drawn between myself and my parents. That definitely became more of a talking point, once I had that record and was on the road to the Olympics. But what surprised me the most was how my mom reacted. She began to tell me that I was going to be better than she ever was. I didn't understand what she meant: I had only gotten this one record. But where I wasn't giving myself credit was the *way* that it happened. In the span of two years, I went from working hard to hit 55s in competition to running a 51. I didn't get there by becoming more efficient—I still had so far to go with learning actual technique. But I had speed. What she meant was that I still had so much to grow into.

Especially when I was starting out, I needed that belief. I needed her to believe in me, I needed a coach who believed in me. Later, I would learn to believe in myself and be able to work with coaches with different styles, but then, I needed to know other people thought I had potential. Having people who really see you for who you truly are reminds you that you can't give up just because one day doesn't go your way. It's okay to admit you need other people believing in you.

The next few months would be a whirlwind: from Nationals for collegiate track and field, I'd go to Nationals for Canada, Olympic trials, then to Rio for the 2016 Olympics... all the while taking summer courses because when I signed up for them, I had no idea this was all about to happen. It all just happened so fast that I didn't really have time to pause and reflect. That came much later.

SPRINT THROUGH YOUR SETBACKS JOURNAL PROMPTS

Grab a notebook or just jot your ideas down on these pages!

FIND YOUR POWER-UP

If someone says something discouraging to you, how do you turn that into ammunition rather than letting it get you down? This could mean creating a 'reset' plan—repeating a mantra five times, listening to a certain pump-up song, anything that can get you back into the zone! Write it down:

My mantra is:

My pump-up music is:

PREP FOR THE WORST CASE

If you tend to be someone who gets stressed out before big events because you're thinking about everything that can go wrong, try this exercise: imagine a big event, whether it's a school project, job interview, race or competition. Now, picture 5 to 7 'worst case scenarios.' Think of things that might go wrong that are stressing you out. After you've made that list, go back and for each scenario, write out exactly how you could handle it to take control of the situation. This way, you're prepared for some of the things that might go wrong, but more importantly, you've shown yourself that even in worst case scenarios, there are ways to get through them! Doing this for any situation that has you stressed helps you become more adaptable and resilient, because it helps build that problem-solving mindset and muscle.

Worst case scenario #1:

I can troubleshoot/control this situation by:

1)

2)

3)

Worst case scenario #2:

I can troubleshoot/control this situation by:

1)

2)

3)

Worst case scenario #3:

I can troubleshoot/control this situation by:

1)

2)

3)

Worst case scenario #4:

I can troubleshoot/control this situation by:

1)

2)

3)

Worst case scenario #5:

I can troubleshoot/control this situation by:

1)

2)

3)

SAVOR YOUR VICTORIES

Ask yourself: How do you celebrate your victories? If you're like me, you likely end up going instantly on to the next thing rather than savoring the moment. But you deserve a celebration when you have a great race, nail the presentation, or get the job. So right now, let's brainstorm a few different ways to celebrate—at different price points, for different levels of 'hooray!' moments.

Free to $5 (Example: a spa night at home giving yourself a manicure and watching a cheesy movie)

- Option 1:
- Option 2:
- Option 3:

$10-$30 (Example: getting your favorite takeout on the way home)

- Option 1:
- Option 2:
- Option 3:

$50+ (Example: dinner at a fancy restaurant, taking the whole team out for ice cream, getting a facial, manicure or blowout)

- Option 1:
- Option 2:
- Option 3:

THINK AHEAD TO WHAT MIGHT BE NEXT

This result at Regionals kicked off a whirlwind that didn't end until I was back in school the next fall after going to the Olympics. I had no idea it was going to be as hectic as it was, but in hindsight, I could have seen it coming and been more prepared for it. The same thing happens when you get accepted to a college or you get the job after a terrifying interview: so often, we see the end goal as getting the job or hitting that one result and we forget to look a little further ahead.

So, look at a couple of your current goals in your life:

- What would it look like if you did accomplish them?
- What could happen when you hit them?
- What might be next?
- Is there anything you should be preparing for now?

You might be surprised at how thinking about what could be next leads you to dream bigger and close in on those current goals even faster.

IMPOSTER

RIO OLYMPICS | BRAZIL | 2016

"Don't wait until you've reached your goal to be proud of yourself. Be proud of every step you take toward reaching that goal."
— Simone Biles

As the daughter of two record-holding Olympians, you may be wondering how I could possibly have Imposter Syndrome—that feeling that no matter what you do, what you accomplish, you must just be faking it and surely someone will call you out. Or maybe, you're wondering how it would be possible for me to avoid it in my situation. If you're thinking the latter, you're right. Anything I could do on the track, other than winning a silver or gold medal at the Olympics or setting *multiple* world records, would be less than their accomplishments, at least on paper. So when I found myself on the sidelines at Rio despite being on the Olympic team, I was deep in Imposter Syndrome, feeling like I didn't belong and that I was just faking it—so much so that it almost ended my track career entirely.

When you have two parents who've represented their countries at the Olympic Games five times in total, it's hard to hear that yes, you're in Rio, you're at the Games, you're representing your country, you've been warming up with the team, you're ready to race… But you're an alternate, and you're not being selected to compete on the day.

On the heels of my 51.97 400-meter run at Regionals, I had a decent but not noteworthy collegiate NCAA National Championships and came sixth in the Canadian Olympic Track and Field Trials. It was a whirlwind summer, so when I got selected to be part of the four by 400-meter relay team for the 2016 Olympics, I barely had a second to bask in the feeling of being invited to my first Olympic team. In retrospect, I wish I had taken more time to enjoy that feeling, because it was about to become a roller coaster of emotions.

Because I was still in school, I had that to keep me distracted through the summer as all of this racing was happening. I took summer classes to have a lighter academic load in 2017 for the collegiate racing season, but when I made that decision, I had no idea that the Olympics would be on my radar. I'd only been to one international competition and while I knew I was running well and I was feeling confident, that was a recent sensation and I didn't know how long it would last.

First, there was the NCAA Nationals. Heading into that race, I was ranked fourth in our conference thanks to my performance at Regionals. Nationals were at this historic track spot in Oregon, Hayward Field. I remember walking in and seeing my name on the board, because they print everybody's name who made it to the NCAAs that year. It felt incredible: I couldn't believe I was there, looking at my name in print. Looking at history.

But I'd had a really long season that year, and I got into my head about how I wasn't feeling great. Running my personal best at Regionals, I felt like I had used up all of my adrenaline. I mentally felt like I was already good, I had done what I set out to do for the year—and that's a dangerous thing to think, because that's when you stop pushing. It was like somewhere in my head, there was a voice telling me, 'one great performance is fine. You're good. You made it to Nationals, so you hit your goal.'

I guess part of me hadn't expected to make it to Nationals at all, so just being there felt like the goal had been achieved. Running the Olympic standard at Regionals had barely sunk in as relevant to what was coming next.

And all of that led to a pretty lackluster race. I didn't make it past the semifinals. It was a little disappointing, but I didn't even have time to think about it before immediately shifting focus to Canadian Championships, and ultimately, the Olympics. It was just one thing after another: there was just enough time to get home, train for a couple weeks, then toe the line at the next Championship race.

I came home to another challenge and mini-drama playing in the background. Coming back to Canada, I shifted to working with a Canadian coach from my old club team in Toronto like I did every summer, but I was still consulting with my coach at the University of Maryland. There was so much noise from both of them that it almost felt as though I didn't have any coach, because there was so much confusion between the two. It doesn't seem like that long ago, but in 2016, coaches weren't yet doing things like Zoom conferences or Google Meets—maybe if it was a few years later, the communication would have been easier, but then, it was me talking to each of them individually, then trying to make a combined plan based on both of their separate inputs. I don't think we ever had one meeting all together or that they ever talked to each other. It's not their fault, it wasn't anyone's responsibility but my own. But at that point, I was young in my career. So I thought, 'Oh, this is going to be fine.' Nope. It wasn't.

Every workout suddenly had a lot of adjustments, the coaches were not really seeing eye to eye, and both wanted me to be doing different things. I was only 21, and I wasn't well versed in how to advocate for myself. I just went along with it and felt like I was the tennis ball in a match, bounced back and forth.

This was the summer I learned that you have to set yourself up for success. No one is going to do that for you.

Still, with the resources I had, I did the best I could. It was busy, and it was complicated. My summer coach—the one at home—wanted me to race in the weeks leading up to the Canadian Championship race. In hindsight, those feelings I had at NCAA Nationals should have meant taking some time to recover, maybe train rather than race. But he didn't really know how Nationals had played out, and my collegiate coach didn't have as much say in my schedule, especially if I wanted to make the Olympic team.

After three weeks of big races and bigger workouts, I went to Canadian Championships already feeling exhausted. I still remember the feeling of being tired on the line... and that's never a good thing. You never want to be tired before even starting to run. There I was in Edmonton, and I was wavering between being absolutely exhausted but also overconfident. I was going into the race as the second fastest woman in Canada and feeling like it was my race.

It wasn't a great race. I narrowly made it through semifinals, but barely.

Suddenly, I was no longer the golden girl of track, I was racing for my life. I had made the finals, which meant I still had a shot at the Olympic team—I remember girls crying after that race because they didn't make it into the last round—so I was happy about that, but I was also incredibly aware that I was struggling, that I had to stop feeling too confident and get focused.

In the finals, I underestimated the energy of the other runners, how they would perform simply because we were in these Olympic Trials. The Trials bring out the best in people, they make you push just a little harder. But as a collegiate runner on top of being an elite runner, I'd already spent those peak performance days, so my energy wasn't matching theirs.

I don't remember much about that race, just seeing everyone pass me and coming in sixth. To make matters worse for me, another girl ran a 52.0 in that race, hitting the Olympic standard. I had been banking on my standard keeping me in the running, but suddenly, I was no longer the only one who'd hit it.

I went back to the hotel that night feeling like everyone was pitying me. The team selection would be announced via email the next day, and I had no idea what to expect. I hadn't run poorly enough to be discounted entirely, but there was no guarantee either. I was up all night waiting for the email, unsure whether I'd be going home on the plane the next day ecstatic because I made it or devastated because I didn't.

The email came.

I barely wanted to open in. But I clicked on it. I didn't make it into the 400-meter individual. The girl who ran the standard in Finals got the third slot to go and run the 400 in Rio, thanks to her performance.

But it wasn't over. I *was* going to the Olympics as part of the relay team. Relays are uncertain, though: I wasn't exactly an alternate, but I wasn't guaranteed the chance to run, since there are 400-meter individual runners who might end up running in the relay as well. Still, the probability of me running was reasonable, so I chose to be thrilled.

What people don't realize is how fast you go from trying to qualify for the Olympics at Olympic Trials to packing your bags and heading to the race location. I'd run under the Olympic standard at Regionals, but I still needed to get through the Olympic Trials at the end of June in Canada to qualify and actually make the team, so it hadn't been a sure thing. After the Trials, once you found out if you were selected, it was basically time to start packing to get to Rio with plenty of time before the racing started. You go from not being an Olympian to putting on your team kit so quickly—it feels so strange, because you expect the process to be much slower, much more ceremonial. But it's really just logistically demanding.

Canadian Championships are three weeks from the time before you leave for the Olympics. So you race, you find out if you're made the team, and then you have only that amount of time to celebrate. In fact, you aren't really even encouraged to celebrate because it's immediately like, 'Hey, get your head in the game, prepare for the Olympics where you will be expected to perform.' So you expect it to be a celebration, but it ends up muted.

When we got to Rio, early in our training there, I ended up getting put into a runoff with another girl who'd made the team, which is just a head-to-head race. So many people simply said they wouldn't do the run-off, and some of the other athletes hadn't arrived yet, so they didn't participate. It was such a strange experience. The coaches made it seem like it didn't matter much and was just a training exercise, but at the same time, it clearly was an important thing to participate in. I had no idea what it would mean, or that it meant anything at all, I just thought I was being a good team player by participating.

I didn't win the run-off.

But in that moment, it didn't seem like a major issue. It just seemed like a minor setback and a chance to have run all out for the first time since arriving. Surely that run-off couldn't be the determining factor whether or not I'd be picked to run in the Olympic relay, I thought. I had a whole season of consistent results and improvements. But the feelings of doubt started to creep in.

Being a track and field athlete in the Olympic village is a surreal experience, because our sport happens during the second half of the 16 days the Olympics are held. Some athletes are finishing while others are just waiting to race. I was torn between wanting to make the absolute most of this experience by being at some of the events and basking in living in the Olympic village, but also wanting to take care of myself to be as prepared as possible for the race. And while going to events doesn't seem like it would be taxing or tiring, the whole vibration of the Games is so intense. There is heightened security everywhere you go, travel to and from venues take a long time and just being at events makes you feel the adrenaline and start getting nervous that you're using too much energy that could better spent on preparing for your own event... especially if you're still not sure if you're racing or not! It's as though all of your senses are heightened during that time and your body is on constant alert. With my event being one of the last in the Games, I had a lot of time to waffle between wanting to stay ready versus enjoying the moment.

I did go watch a tennis match since tennis was my first love and for most of my time growing up, my plan had been to be the next Serena Williams, not the next Florence Griffith Joyner (the track star you probably know as Flo-Jo). Plus, watching tennis felt so far removed from track and field events that it took my mind off of the waiting. Waiting is even worse when you don't know if you're racing, because you have no idea how to set your expectations. Do you let yourself feel excited and risk being disappointed, or do you assume you're not running and risk being either completely flat or over-excited on race day if you get selected?

It felt like everyone around me was just so composed and in their own focused zone. I'm sure they were all internally freaking out, but even knowing that, I didn't know how to interact with everyone. I kept thinking, 'I'm excited, but I don't want to be too excited. Should I be really quiet and reserved and look like I'm super focused? Will that stand out to the other athletes and the coach? If I look like I'm enjoying myself and having fun, will they think I'm not taking it seriously?'

Yes, I was overthinking it way too much. I started to feel like everyone was judging how I was acting, and that they were thinking that I wasn't worthy of being on the team.

And yes, I know that's just me projecting. None of them cared. I have no idea what they were really thinking.

But it was my first Olympic team. And I had this image in my head of how Olympic athletes act.

This is where the Imposter Syndrome comes in: you make it to the big race, and you're still feeling like you're just playing a part and you need to decide who to act like, because obviously, you can't just be yourself. Mentally, I was trying to keep my head in the game. Canada expects a certain amount of medals, and if I ran, I wanted that podium. I wanted to be contributing.

You might assume that we would find out if we were running at least a day before your race, right? That's not how it works when you're one of the potential runners on the team. Everything is up in the air until race day, especially with this particular race because the 400-meter hurdles happen earlier on race day, so some of the runners from that *may* be on the team, but may be having a bad day, may get injured during their run, or may just not be feeling good after their race. They aren't guaranteed to be able to run, even if they're the coach's top pick. The same is true of anyone who ran the individual 400 earlier. Maybe they made it through the semifinals, but didn't have a good race in the quarterfinals. Basically, you're trying to put together a team based on who's the freshest, healthiest, and has the best chance of performing, but you're waiting for other results in order to determine that. It makes sense on paper, but it's really hard on runners like me who've been brought along solely to race the relay. For us, it's our one chance to race in the Olympics and the waiting is agony.

So, the morning of the semifinals race, I went downstairs, got my bib number and accreditation, ate breakfast as though I was gearing up for the run of my life, and left with the team for the stadium for round one. The relay is actually a two-day event. First, Canada needs a relay team to get through the semifinals and get into the finals. For that team, the coaches selected all runners who had competed at the Olympics before. The goal isn't to put in your full team for the finals, it's just to have a good enough team to *make* the finals. I thought to myself, 'Okay, you don't necessarily have to put your best people in, you just want to put enough people that have good legs to get you in the final.' I figured, 'They're running people with experience. Let them start us off strong that way.'

Thankfully, Canada made it through to the finals. I still hadn't run, but I still had a chance of running the finals—which, by the way, were the last track and field event of the Games. No pressure.

The next morning, we had another team meeting where we started talking about who would run in the finals. The team captain said that we should put fresh legs on the team. I knew she was in my corner and wanted to advocate for me to run, in part because she knew that Team Jamaica and Team USA were going to be using that strategy. But the head coach wasn't convinced. He thought it should actually be the team that ran well in the semis. We went to the track that morning for what would be our final practice, with the goal of finalizing the team who would be running that night. On the shuttle bus, one of the girls who had been on the semis team was talking to me, and she was saying that she wasn't feeling very good—she'd fallen during a hurdle practice—and she told me she thought I'd be taking her place. Essentially, she was saying, "Get ready."

In my head, I was doing cartwheels. I was thinking, 'Oh my gosh. It's go time. This is my moment. It's amazing.' At practice, I did all of my drills with this excitement in the air, just waiting to hear my name in the lineup, seeing myself on the start line, visualizing taking the baton and running Canada to a gold.

We get called into the huddle. The coach started going through the lineup. I'll never forget, he named every single person's name who was going to run and not me.

The only name not called.

I felt like I was in a nightmare flashback to elementary school where teams are getting picked in gym class and it's not even that you're the last name called, you're just not called at all and you're left standing alone while all the other kids run over to start the game.

In that moment, I questioned everything. Why did I come? Why am I here? What was the point?

Luckily, my mom was there. I hadn't seen her much all week, since she wanted me to have the experience of being in the moment with the team. But she was there in the stadium. I excused myself, then climbed up the steps to find her, and we sat together as we watched the girls warm up. I can't remember if I cried or not. I just knew I was devastated and I wasn't sure what the sport could mean to me going forward. I felt lost. My mom—and I'll tell more stories about her later—was a rock. She didn't offer advice as a former Olympian, she didn't offer advice as my mom. She just sat quietly with me, silently offering support. Just being there was the best thing she could do for me in that moment.

I had my moment with her where the feelings washed over me, but I also was aware that I would need to snap out of it. Yes, I was upset. But while I wanted to just hang up my track spikes and fly home and the last thing I wanted to do was rejoin my teammates as the girl who didn't get to run, the little voice in the back of my head was telling me, 'You don't want to end your career or the Games like this.'

I knew if I wanted to continue on the track, I needed to be supportive of the girls and celebrate the fact that they had an amazing race. I knew I wanted to be part of that in the future and that being dramatic and upset about it outwardly in that moment could jeopardize that. And the girls who did run didn't deserve to have someone bringing down their energy.

Did I feel like it should have been me out there? Yes. And I did eventually actually have a chat with the head coach a year later, where I felt brave enough to ask him why he didn't choose me. It was a hard question to ask because I wasn't sure I even wanted to know the answer, but I also knew that if I wanted to make another Olympic team, I needed to know if there was something that I could control that would help me.

And he apologized. He didn't say he made the wrong decision, but he said that at the time, he felt as though it was the right decision to go with more experienced runners. Looking back, he saw that there may have been other options. I think he just thought that at 21, I was too young and too new to the sport. It was only my second international meet at that point. I hadn't had the best Nationals. I'd run the standard at Regionals, but since then, my season had been on a downward trend. I didn't make it an easy decision for him—and that's what I learned in that moment. You want to be the one selected to run? Make it an easy decision for the coach to make. You want to get that sponsorship from your favorite brand? Make it an easy decision for them.

Imposter Syndrome is really you blaming yourself for not being where you want to be, or not feeling like you belong there once you are in the room. But how can you take responsibility for that feeling and ask yourself how you can change the narrative? How can you take ownership for your situation in a way that's productive?

Looking back at the decision the coach made to not put me in, I can see where he was coming from. Of course, I wish he'd thought about it differently, but if I want to learn from it and make sure it doesn't happen again, I need to own what I can about the situation.

So, looking at it from an outsider's perspective: I ran the Olympic standard in May. Then, I figured that was great, and it was going to carry into the Trials at the end of June. So by the time the Trials rolled around, I had not run that standard in well over a month. I was also a little burned out and over-raced, and it was showing in my performances. I hadn't yet built up any type of consistency in my runs. I was usually running the 400 meter in the high 52s, not the high 51s. If I was a coach, I would see that. I wouldn't be looking for one incredible result, I'd be looking for a history of solid results. When I could see my racing from that perspective, I could see the clear path to what I needed to do to make the team: I didn't just need one result, I needed to build consistency in my results.

Coming home, I did feel like an imposter. The whole Games experience felt weird. Going from feeling certain I was going to get to run to watching from the stands is just about the most extreme way to feel Imposter Syndrome. But at the same time, I wouldn't change how I prepared. If I had come to the Games with the mindset that I might not run, if I had warmed up in that practice as though I wasn't getting selected, then of course I wouldn't have gotten the chance to run. You can't let the fear of not getting picked keep you from putting yourself out there.

I felt like I had been making such big leaps and bounds in track, so to have that feel like it was taken away from me stung. I knew I would have to go back to school and contend with people asking about the Olympics. I'd have to say that yes, I was there, I was chosen for the team, I'm an Olympian. But no, I didn't run. People I knew from track had apparently set up watch parties for me, they were ready to cheer me on. They didn't get that chance and I felt guilty about it. It was tough answering those questions and it was even harder explaining something that I wasn't entirely sure that I understood.

But those friends weren't judging me. They supported me. They reminded me that no matter what happened, I had made the Olympic team. That's pretty much as high as it gets when it comes to track. If anything, the track team was excited to have an

Olympian on the team and I think it inspired us to really get down to business that year.

It stayed with me, though, that I made the team but I didn't run. There were these moments of joy, like getting my Olympic ring in the mail and holding that and knowing that it was this tangible proof that I had made it. But there were also moments where I didn't feel like I was part of it—I even skipped the banquet held for Canadian Olympians a couple months later because I was away at school and couldn't get back easily. I had considered going, but all I could imagine was feeling awkward because everyone else had raced.

It's tempting to have that moment be the moment where your story ends. I didn't get picked, so it's over. And there was a second where I considered it. But racing track teaches you that there are going to be so many setbacks. Some are big, some are tiny, but they're always going to happen. This was a setback. It was a big one. But you have to trust the process and trust that you're going to get through this setback to get to the thing that really is for you. I've never been the person to just stay sitting on the bleachers.

The thing with Imposter Syndrome is that for most of us, it's never going to go away entirely. You might not feel it for a while, but it's always lurking, waiting for the moment when you're feeling down. As I navigated a hamstring injury in 2023, as I was trying to put in my prep for the 2024 Olympic Trials, it reared its ugly head again. With the 400-meter run having such a deep field now, it takes a lot to make it. And I'm still waiting to have 'my race'—the race that really represents all the work I've been doing. Because at practice, I feel amazing. But I haven't managed to have the result I'm looking for at an international meet. I'm still looking for the time that will make me feel like that world class 400-meter runner. I've had a taste of it: running school records, going to the Olympics, winning on the Commonwealth Games relay team. I'm 90 percent there, but that last 10 percent... I'm still waiting for that.

I know I have a race in me that's going to make me truly, truly, truly have that *aha* moment and believe in my talent and all the work I've done—but I'm still waiting. And I'm not sure I'll ever get there, because there's always going to be another race, another goal. Maybe that's okay—in fact, maybe Imposter Syndrome is there to show you what you really want, to remind you that there's always going to be more. There's always going to be a next level to aim for, and if you didn't have that kind of goal to go after, what would be the point?

There are sayings like 'feeling like a hamster on a wheel,' or 'feeling like you're stuck on a treadmill.' Being a professional runner is like that. In most other professional sports, like tennis or soccer or hockey, there's a clear pathway and it's apparent when you're a professional and when you're an amateur. It's clear when you've 'made it.' When you're a professional in those sports, you have teams and coaches and managers in charge of your scheduling and putting you in certain tournaments. In running, there's no blueprint. You can be an elite or professional racer, but you may not have an agent or a manager. You can have the fast times, but you may not have the resources to get over to Europe to race. You may have a sponsor one year, and they're gone the next. You're always feeling like it could go away at any moment. Because of that, it's impossible to not feel like an imposter in the sport sometimes.

But now, I try to use Impostor Syndrome as a starting point. I let it show me where I want to be, and what I need to do to get there. I feel like I don't belong on this Olympic team? Great. What can I do that will make me feel like I belong? What steps can I take? I think it's okay to acknowledge that Imposter Syndrome is going to come up throughout our lives. But I also don't think it should define you: You can use it to help you see who you really want to be, what you really want to achieve, and then, make a plan to get there.

SPRINT THROUGH YOUR SETBACKS JOURNAL PROMPTS

Grab a notebook or just jot your ideas down on these pages!

IDENTIFY IMPOSTER SYNDROME IN YOUR LIFE

Most of us have experienced Imposter Syndrome at some point in our lives—it's almost unavoidable! Can you think of times where you felt like you were completely in over your head and faking it? Make a list! (Example: A school presentation, the start line at a race, or starting a new internship.)

1.
2.
3.
4.
5.

NAME YOUR IMPOSTER SYNDROME

Imposter Syndrome shows up as a voice in your head telling you that you're not worthy. Rather than thinking of it as part of you, why not give her a name? I like to look at Imposter Syndrome as an annoying old friend who occasionally shows up at my door. Having her be her own separate entity helps me see those negative thoughts for what they are—thoughts that don't serve me, that aren't representative of who I truly am.

START YOUR DAY RIGHT

Every morning, first thing when you get up, write down one thing you're proud of. It can be the tiniest accomplishment ever, or something really big. So many of us wake up and scroll through our phones immediately, and by doing that, we're instantly comparing ourselves to other people and often end up feeling less-than because of it. Starting a morning 'accomplishment list' will help you see just how much progress you actually make in a week, a month or a year! (Bonus points if you can come up with more than one thing each morning, but starting with one is a great spot.)

GET RATIONAL

From that list, pick 1-5 examples you wrote down, and make a chart with three columns. In the first column, write down each example. In the next column, for each example, write another sentence or two about why you felt like an imposter. What about the situation made you feel like you weren't ready, or were faking it? And finally, in the third column, write down why that feeling isn't accurate—or what you could do to make sure it isn't accurate in the future!

For example, if your Imposter Syndrome came before doing a presentation to your class because you felt like you weren't a good speaker, are there examples of times where you have given a good presentation? Or are there things you could have done, like practicing your presentation with some friends, that would have helped make you feel prepared?

This is a great exercise to show you that when you actually calm down and think critically about your Imposter Syndrome, it's either inaccurate or it's providing some information you can work with so you're ready for next time.

IMPOSTER SYNDROME MOMENT	WHY YOU FEEL LIKE AN IMPOSTER	WHY THAT'S WRONG and/or HOW YOU CAN SHIFT YOUR MINDSET

HAVE YOUR POSITIVE AFFIRMATION TOOLKIT

On your phone, cultivate a Positive Affirmation Toolkit that reminds you of who you want to be, what you want to do, and the greatness that is you. I have a favorites folder with things like a video of my best race ever and pictures of me with my Olympic ring and different medals I've won. I also have a note in my Notes app that has some positive affirmations and goals for myself, plus a 'positive vibes' playlist I can turn on when I need the extra pick-me-up. Build the toolkit when you're in a good mood, and it'll help you in those tough moments. Having those videos and photos, that accomplishment list, those notes to yourself... those can help stop Imposter Syndrome in its tracks!

CHOOSE "I GET TO" VERSUS "I HAVE TO"

Imposter Syndrome can show up as the feeling that you are stuck doing something... even when it's something that you used to love doing! In high school, I loved how running felt. I just loved the racing and the going to meets, regardless of how I performed. Now that I'm older, it's easy to feel negative about a training day that wasn't perfect. But when I reframe it and remind myself that I get to do this as a career, it helps me see an imperfect practice as an opportunity for growth, not a problem.

CONSISTENCY

"Don't sit down and wait for the opportunities to come. Get up and make them."
—Madam C.J. Walker

My mindset is all about focusing on the big picture—but at the same time, breaking my big picture goals down into the small actions that I can be taking right now in order to manifest the future that I want. At the moment when I'm writing this book, that looks like dealing with an injury before I can think about competing for that 2024 Paris Olympic berth, and it's made me think a lot about the power of self-belief in both the long-term and the short-term.

You want everything to go exactly how you want it to, *right now*. But sometimes you have to take these side roads that lead to the big goal. Having an injury is hard. When I look at the big picture, I know that almost a year ahead of the Games is the best possible time in the lead up to the Olympics to be dealing with an injury, because I have the time to deal with it and I can be more patient. I know what I need to work on and I'm not trying to rush the process. But I don't think always having a positive mindset is something that comes naturally for anyone. It's something you have to work on. For me, I was lucky that I had my mom as a role model. Raising me as a single mom who still had her own big goals, I got to see firsthand how she made everything seem possible. She never doubted.

A lot of people meet me and think that because I'm really smiley, I'm a super positive person. And I love that—but it's been a work in progress. I had a breakdown before my run on a random Saturday because I knew my hamstring wasn't feeling amazing. I was sitting there sobbing, feeling sorry for myself. And I had to shake it off, because if I keep making excuses or keep finding the things that are wrong with the situation, it can lead to seemingly endless negativity. I know that I can be so hard on myself. I have to flip those thoughts. I had to have a conversation with myself: 'What's future Micha going to say? She's going to be so proud of you if you go out there and do what you can.'

When I think about Future Micha, I feel a camaraderie with her. I feel like she's part of my team. These individual sports can feel lonely if you let them. I remember racing the in the 4 x 400-meter relay at the Commonwealth Games in 2022: I was running and getting ready to pass off the baton to the next girl, and I had this moment where I was so aware that I felt like I was running so free and easy and it was as if I was already embodying my future self, saying, 'This feels right. This feels easy.' And in that moment, I knew that the better I positioned myself in that lap, the better the future would look for me.

I look back and realize that in the past, I often gave myself the best chance for the opportunities that I have today. I can thank my past self for that—and try to best serve my future self in the current moment. Future Micha is the truest version of myself, with this quiet confidence and ease that I can continue to aspire to.

I love taking the "why not me?" approach. You have to have these audacious, awesome thoughts. For me back in 2012, that was "What if I make the Olympic team?" I had no business saying that at the time, but why *shouldn't* it be me? I know I'm lucky that I've had people around me to model that: both my mom and dad achieved so much in their athletic careers. But even if you don't have that directly around you, you just have to look online to find examples of people who've done amazing things, people who are just like you. Personally, I love seeing other people on social media achieving big goals because it reminds me that it's possible. I'm drawn to people with high goals, rather than falling into comparison with them.

Getting to those goals starts with stripping away everything that isn't serving you. When things get heavy, when things feel hard, rather than asking what I can add into my life in order to fix a situation, I try to ask what I can take out. How can I simplify things? How can I take it down to the bare minimum? Usually, overwhelm is what's making a situation worse, whether it's injury or struggling to meet a certain goal—and if you can simplify down to the essentials, it all starts to feel more manageable again.

For me, the simplest way to look at track is this: whoever gets to the line first gets rewarded. So how do I run fast enough to be that person? It's amazing how that simple question can clarify so much —even if you think you were already doing everything right, sometimes you're doing too much.

I think you do have to learn it on your own through repetition, but what I've realized is that every time you step up to the line, you're going to feel doubts. And every time, you can catch them in that moment, and then remind yourself that you've been in this place before and made it through, therefore you can do it again. You can put all the noise to the side and say, "I'm here. I'm here for a reason. Let's do it."

After making the team but not getting to run at Rio, when I reflected on why I wasn't chosen, I kept coming back to the fact that I hadn't yet proved I could be consistent. Imposter Syndrome would creep in often after that moment in Rio, especially once I was finished with racing collegiate track and was going all-in on being a professional runner. Whenever I did have those moments, though, I would remind myself to focus on what I could control and what would get me onto the next Olympic team.

I still wanted to run more personal bests but I knew that the more important thing to focus on was my consistency. Before I focused on hitting a low 51-second 400-meter run, I was going to need to dial in my ability to hit 52s in every race.

In the 2021 season, I was finally there. It had been five years since my personal best at Regionals in Jacksonville and I hadn't hit that time since then. I made the transition to being a professional runner after college, but struggled to find my stride. I felt like I was always swinging back and forth—I'd have a great race, then a bad one. I was continuously second-guessing my approach, worrying more about how the coach would interpret my race versus putting in my best effort. I needed to find the right rhythm again.

I used to think, 'If I don't run fast, then I'm not going to be considered for this team. And then I'm not going to be taken seriously. And then this is going to get back to the Olympic committee or the committee that determines who gets carding—government funding for athletes—and it's all going to be over.' Every race was therefore make-or-break, and that was making me miserable.

I had to shift that narrative and stay in the moment at races. I needed to be as prepared and dialed in as possible, and let my legs do the talking on race days. That meant overhauling my approach to racing, from how I was going to sleep the night before to how I actually approached the 52 seconds of performance on the track.

I had the tendency to think too much in races when I was a younger runner. I'd have a start that wasn't great—not bad, just not amazing—and instantly, I'd be in my head. That's the worst way to approach a 400-meter run, since so much can happen in the last 100 meters. As long as you're within striking distance of a competitor, you're still running to win. No matter what, you can't count yourself out. I know that I may not have the best start—but I *can* have the best finish, so I began to focus on how to hone that last 200 meters. How could I turn on the afterburners and have the strongest finish possible? When it comes to being competitive, that's what brings out the best in me: being able to chase someone is better for me than running in first and being chased. It's more motivating. And it means that I can never count myself out, even if I'm sitting in last with 100 meters to go. Making the decision to be that kind of runner gave me the ability to start pushing to eke out that extra second in any race situation.

Consistency on the track is so, so specific. Hitting a 51 versus a 52 versus a 53 is so different. It takes an intense amount of focus and preparation and so much awareness of your body and where you are in space during a race, which has to also translate to how you perform in practice. And it messes with your head, because unlike team sports or longer distance runs where a few seconds or minutes off is normal in practice and even in racing, on the track, milliseconds matter. It's also more repeatable than any other sport, since it's the same track every time. You're not on a different race course or playing a different team, you're just running on the same type of turf for under a minute. Every time.

This allows you to learn to be incredibly consistent, but it can also box you in.

I knew running consistently was what I struggled to do, so I started journaling on how I could be more consistent if I had any hope of making my next Olympic team. I started writing about how I needed to believe in myself at every single practice and to be intentional every time I showed up to the track. Teaching myself consistency would mean that I couldn't phone anything in. Everything needed to be dialed. Consistent and committed had to become my watch words for the year, in every area of my life.

I needed to sleep more and be more careful about my bedtime. I needed to prioritize drinking electrolytes and a protein shake after every session at the gym or on the track. And on the track, every workout needed to be done with absolute dedication and intention. I needed to start fighting to hit the low end of my time ranges in intervals. This sounds a little weird, but if you do a track workout, you usually have a distance, like 200 meters, and a time range for how fast you'll run it, like 28 to 32 seconds. In the past, I may not have stressed about finishing each rep around 32 seconds. But now? Aiming for 28 became the new goal. Consistency became about consistently pushing for the better result, reaching for a little bit higher every time.

Everything was a chance to practice consistency, to get just a little bit better. My first collegiate coach would always tell us, "If you're early, you're on time. If you're on time, you're late. If you're late, don't bother coming." And I still hold on to that. That as my starting point helped a lot in terms of training and having that discipline when I go to practice.

Every time I went to the gym or the track, I got intentional. What am I working on? What's the goal? Is it that I'm going to make sure I get out strong on every single rep no matter what? If so, that's it. That's all I'm focusing on. If it's about technique, that has my full attention.

You do this enough times, and you realize that you're finally tapping into your full potential.

My coach used to say, "Leave whatever is on your mind outside of the track and just put your attention into this workout." In college, that meant forgetting about the petty arguments I was having with teammates or roommates or worrying about a class. Now, it meant forgetting about if I was going to get funding or get selected for the next international meet. The only thing that mattered when I walked into the track was that day's workout.

The same thing applies to races: I had to get intentional about each of those as well. At first, I worried that writing out intentions for a race would make me stressed out and I'd get in my own head about it. But in reality, I just needed to rethink how I was forming my intentions. Yes, times matter, but in races, setting a time goal isn't really enough—you need more of a 'how' to go with the 'what.' So I started making intentions for races like getting out really strong on the first 100 meters, staying in contact with at least one other runner who started in front of me, or coming into the last lap really pumping my arms—details that I could focus on that would get me to my time goal.

This isn't manifesting or practicing something you've read in *The Secret*. It's not like you just close your eyes and if you believe it enough, you'll run fast. You write down 'get out strong' as your intention for your workouts, practice that often enough that it comes naturally when you're writing it down and heading to the track on race day. Your body gets used to it, because you've practiced. And you've been able to practice it and embody it fully because you've journaled on it over and over. By the time you're in a race, you're ready to be consistent. You have a strong start, because that's what you've practiced. You stay in contact with the girl who was in the lane next to you, and you're aware of what's happening around you while still focusing on your own race. And you come into the finish pumping your arms and pushing as hard as you can. That's how you create consistency—and it almost always translates into a good time.

Consistency doesn't mean being rigid and needing everything to be perfect in order to perform. It's about controlling the things that you know you can control, not about racing well if everything is exactly right. If you need the weather to be exactly 24 degrees and you need lane four and you need everyone to be quiet at the start and you need everyone to just stay out of your way when you're warming up, that may be your optimal racing situation, but there's no way that you can make that happen every time. That's not controllable. It might be ideal for you, but it's not going to happen at every race. To replicate that would almost be impossible. Your consistency comes from bringing the headphones you need and having your warmup playlist ready so you can prep with minimal interruption. It comes from bringing the right clothing so that you always feel the right level of warmth ahead of the race. It comes from knowing exactly how to handle every lane, so that if you're assigned your favorite one, it's a benefit rather than a necessity. It comes from tuning out the noise on the start line, letting it flow over you but not distract you from the task at hand. And your consistency also comes from everything you've done leading up to that race day. Have you been consistent in your approach before race day?

My race day routine has been honed over the years. I lay out my clothes the day before, especially if I'm sharing a hotel room since you don't want to be a bad roommate digging for your stuff early in the morning. What I'm going to wear depends on the race, so I make sure that I have the right clothing laid out. My competition clothing is different from what I wear in most practices, but I love that because it's a little sign to my brain when I put those clothes on that it's time to get serious. When that kit goes on, it's the 'real effort' day. By putting that kit out the night before, I'm already putting that energy out there and starting to get that feeling of being ready to race. I'll also spend some time with my journal, going over the plan for the next day, writing out my race intentions.

I usually watch some kind of really light, easy movie or show before I go to bed, just to try to keep myself in a calm mood—you don't want to get overstimulated the night before a race. That usually means watching something goofy or even a reality show. On race morning, I wake up at least four hours before the race—you need that much time in order to be able to eat and digest. So if I race at noon, I wake up at eight. I have oatmeal for breakfast because I've found that it stays down and it will sustain me until the race, without weighing me down. Running the 400 is a really tricky distance for your stomach—mine gets very sensitive! During breakfast, I just look over the race schedule and my plan that I've written down, reviewing it and making sure I know what time I need to be ready. I don't dwell on it, but I do want to double check it. You hear too many horror stories about people missing their start because they had the time wrong!

After breakfast, I put on makeup. Here's the thing: No, you don't need makeup to race. But personally, I feel more powerful and energized by putting on a little bit of makeup, really accentuating my eyes. If I'm going to have a picture or video of me running, I do feel like I stand out more if I've taken a few seconds to put on a bit of makeup and feel my best. It makes me feel more confident and almost sets me up to be in the lead, being photographed. It's sending a message to my brain that I am ready to stand out. I used to not do this. I didn't put any makeup on and do my nails because I was like, 'I don't care. I'm not going to take any extra time to put myself together.' I look back at that version of myself and realize that it wasn't me not caring, it was me not feeling good enough to show up to the start line feeling like my best self. I didn't trust that I would have a good run, and I was scared of what people would think if the slow girl was out there all made up. Putting on makeup now feels like I'm saying to myself and everyone else that I believe I'm going to have a good day. And while I'm there, I give myself a little mirror pep talk. Just 'you've got this.' Nothing fancy. (I should add that I'm also blasting good music, like some 2000s pop with some Destiny's Child, just something that makes me feel happy.)

I do a quick check of my bag after I get dressed and make sure I have my track spikes and my bib number if I've already picked it up. I make sure my water bottle is in there along with my electrolytes, my snacks, a band for stretching, maybe even a book if I know there's going to be a lot of down time before or after the race.

In most events, you can't have your headphones in when you're warming up because there's so much going on on the track, but I still bring my headphones so I can listen to music before and after warmup while waiting around. Getting to the track on time means getting there at least 90 minutes before your race in order to get checked in. Once I'm at the track and it's time to get ready, I just focus on my warmup, which is around an hour and fifteen minutes long.

And then, things get serious. The second part of the check-in process is when you go to the call room, where you will wait until you race. Usually, you can't bring much with you to that spot. I'll usually have just my spikes, and sometimes they let you have a watch but sometimes you can't bring *anything* in because you won't be back in that room again. The watch is nice since you know how much time you have until your race, but you learn to live without it.

Personally, I like to look down and think, 'Alright, I'm racing in 10 minutes. And I'll be done in 11 minutes.' Which is a very weird thought!

Usually, you spend your 15 minutes or so in the call room trying to stay in the zone. It's hard because you're just sitting around, so everyone is usually trying to bounce around a bit, keep moving, keep focused. You kind of get into this trance state if you're not careful. The goal is to be really calm and steady, almost like you're asleep, but really, you're ready to pounce. It's a fine line.

Whether it's a big or a small meet, when it's time to go, you get walked out to the track and taken to your blocks—where your feet are positioned and you push off to get started—that are set up in your lane. You set your blocks the way that you want them, and then you get your hands and feet adjusted the way that works best for you. You give the blocks a couple little tests, just making sure they're stable and you'll be able to push down on them with all your power when the gun goes off. You usually have time for a couple of test starts before you get called back to your blocks to set up for the actual race start.

Once everyone is there, it starts to get quiet. The official tells you to go to your marks, and you step up to your blocks and get yourself set up. The silence intensifies even more. You become aware of everything: your heartbeat, swallowing, breathing... you have a few seconds, and this is where I make myself smile before I look straight ahead and get fully focused.

My personal favorite moment of consistency that sets me up at any race start is this: to make sure that as I get into the blocks and look ahead, I smile. There's nothing better for making you instantly feel calm and ready to go than the act of smiling—and it also lets your competitors know that you are feeling good today. When I look around, I almost never see people smiling, but if they are, I know that they're going to be fast. Smiling on the start line is the most confident thing you can do. If you can do that and you can mean it, you've already won. That's my little ritual, and it makes a big difference.

If you're a runner, you know that being nervous makes you tense, and that makes you run really rigid and tight. So if you can go into a race with a feeling of joy where a smile washes over your body, you're going to do better than if you're grimacing before the race even begins. But now, you're here. This is your moment.

On your mark. You're in the blocks.

Get set. Your hips come up.

Go. You don't wait to hear the whole word. The moment you hear *anything,* you're up and running for all you're worth.

At that point, it's all about the first 50 meters. You're going all out. It's pure adrenaline. You're not thinking, you're just going. There is nothing in your head. You are the race.

After the first 50 meters, you settle into a slight rhythm—which obviously only will last for 30 seconds or so—where you're focusing on your race, but also becoming aware of where people are around you.

At the 300 meter mark—just over 10 seconds to go—is when you begin to feel the pain. And that's when you're screaming in your head to keep pushing. You can stop in 10 seconds.

When you're about to cross the finish line, sometimes people look over their shoulders instinctively, but you're not really supposed to. It can cost you time—or cause you to crash as you come through. I don't look. I'll find out soon enough and there's no point in checking where I am in that moment. Still, it's hard to fight that instinct.

At the end, you want to be on the ground, or at least *feel* like you want to be. Despite every fiber in my body telling me to crawl I try to stay on my feet and fight the lactic build up. My coach at Maryland always told me to never let your competition see you on the ground and to do your best to keep it moving. Remind your body that it'll feel better in a few minutes. And once I'm moving again, I do try to cool down with some movement. It's not always easy because of everything going on around you, but it is really important if you don't want to be sore the next day. I also try to find a minute to jot a few notes down about the race in my journal or on my phone since right after the race is when you have the best memory of what actually happened, what you can work on, anything you need to discuss with your coach, that kind of thing.

My goal in the 2021 season became less about winning and more about having those results stay consistent. It worked. I was finally regularly finishing with 52 times, rather than some 52s, some 54s, maybe a great result with a 51. I wanted a smoother line of results rather than that singular spike up for one great day. It was as if I had this switch just flip on: I'd been running 53s for the past few years with the occasional 52 and I knew I was capable of hitting that 51 again. I was never satisfied with 53. But before I could start hitting 51s, I needed to get consistent about hitting 52s.

I had an opportunity to run a full season in 2021 after being on pause during COVID, struggling to do any real training. I was looking forward to taking every opportunity I could to run fast, and I'd had a great training block thanks to the newfound focus on intentional workouts. I didn't quite expect it to go as well as it did right away, but I started the season with a 52. That set me on fire. I felt a lot more like my old self, the girl who ran that 51.97 at Regionals, not the girl who missed getting to run at the Olympics.

I was running not just with fresh legs and newfound heart, I was running with intention. I was racing like my life depended on getting out a lot stronger in race starts. I narrowly missed the Olympic selection, running the Olympic standard only after the team was already picked. I still had a bit of hope the night the selections were being made since I had been running really well, I just was not an automatic selection. It was a gut punch when the email didn't come. But instead of going back to feeling like I was being left at home, not picked for the team, I doubled down on racing in Canada, taking advantage of getting as much racing exposure as I could get. There was nothing left to lose, and I had nowhere to go other than turning inward.

I raced the Athletics Ontario Open and Para Provincial Championships in early August of 2021, feeling a little lonely since everyone I usually would race or train with was making their final Olympic preparations for Tokyo, which had been bumped from 2020 to 2021 due to the pandemic. Smaller races like this really strip away the complications of being a pro athlete and you go back to those basics. But the real me is going to put myself out there, regardless of how big or small a meet is.

Going into Provincials, I did feel like I was at my home race, like I was in my most comfortable space. My partner was in the stands cheering for me, which happens rarely because of our work and travel schedules. The day just felt fun, and it let me finally feel like I was exhaling and just finding this joy again. We started, and I almost instantly caught up to the girl on the outside of me before the 20 meter mark, putting me in the lead. Strong start, check. I came around the turn alone, and scanning around me, I was way out front. I could hear my breath. I could hear my footfalls. I felt like everything was coming together. I crossed the line in first, feeling like my intentions and my consistency came together perfectly.

It wasn't exactly what I wanted. I wasn't in Tokyo. But my partner was there. My mom was there. And my time was enough to put me in the top six in Canada. If I had run that time a few weeks earlier, I would have been going to Tokyo, but that didn't upset me. I just felt so proud that I didn't give up.

I realized that I needed to own my running and my abilities. I needed to know that I'm somebody who can automatically run a fast time. I had to believe in myself, not wait for permission or for others to believe in me. When I first started running, I needed that external validation that I could do this. But that only gets you so far: you also need to believe in yourself.

It was a good season for me to look back and think, 'Okay, you didn't make an Olympic team. But you had your most consistent season. And yes, the gut punch of not making the team really, really hurt. But I love that I kept going.' I love that I kept running because that ability to keep going is what's going to allow you to stay motivated in those situations where you feel like maybe it's not worth it. Every race is a chance to run better.

A lot of people—even newer track runners—misjudge sprinting and shorter distances. They think that there's no technique involved. They think that it's just running, and then you stop when you cross the line. Anyone can do that, right? But I think to run at a high level consistently, you need to really know your body and know how to use it, when to push a little harder and when to conserve your energy for another second, and to be able to do all of that in milliseconds during a race without getting distracted from the actual run. It may seem like you blink and the race is over. If you haven't watched track racing before, go to YouTube and watch a 400 meter race. It's over so fast, it looks like there's no way the runners are doing anything other than running as hard as they can. But actually, it's so slowed down in your mind as it's happening. You're constantly making minor adjustments in the race. You're constantly trying to ignore pain signals from your body.

And that leads to the other part of consistency, which is a little different: it's about knowing when to *not* race or train rather than pushing through. If I'm injured, then I don't race. If I'm really sick, then I don't race. Racing through injury or illness used to feel like a badge of honor when I was a younger runner, but as I got older, I realized it was actually hurting me. Not only was it making it harder for me to recover and even prolonging injuries, it was tanking my ability to be a consistent runner.

It's a fine line, because you do have to be careful that you're not milking an injury or letting a minor niggle hold you back from performing on an important day. And sometimes, you do have to push through and perform because the race matters that much. You have to make sure that you're not letting your subconscious talk you out of racing because you're scared, getting you to a place where you're rationalizing skipping a race because your knee is sore, even though it's not so bad. You're never going to feel perfect on race day. At Nationals in 2023, I was dealing with a nagging hamstring injury that had been ongoing, but I knew that Nationals was an important race if I wanted to be considered for carding and projects that would let me be considered for the Olympic team. In that race, I came back from seventh place at the 300 meter mark, all the way up to fourth place by the end of the race.

The best part about consistency is that it's something you can work on regardless of what's happening around you or even how well you're running. As I'm working on this book, I'm dealing with medial tibial stress syndrome—basically, an overuse injury in my lower leg—and I'm not running. Instead, I'm wearing a boot and doing physical therapy and cross-training. No, this isn't an ideal situation. But what I can do with it is start to work on consistency in my daily routines. My bedtime and sleep habits had gotten a little more lax. I'd go to bed at nine sometimes and wake up feeling great, but other nights, I'd stay up well past that and be paying for it the next day. That's not consistent, and it's not serving me.

Having the time away from running forced me to go back to the basics, to think about what I could control. That included bedtime. It also included cross-training. I know a lot of athletes who get injured and really struggle to be consistent with their physical therapy or with their cross-training on the bike or in the pool. It's not our normal routine, so it's easy to skip it. It's not as enjoyable for us and it can feel so frustrating, so it's easy to skip it. It's also easy to start feeling like an imposter again: for me, here I am, a professional runner who can't run. It's natural to be feeling down about that. But then I think about the person I want to be. Your presence is how you carry yourself. It's how you think about yourself in any environment. I want to feel strong and maintain that champion mindset, and if I can't do it on the track right now, where else can I do it?

I have to remind myself that when I'm not in the usual track setting, when I'm training at the public gym, there is a lot of good that can still come from that. It's all about how you approach it.

You need your consistency—the routine—and your intention—the mindset—to work in tandem with each other. That's where you start to see real results. It works on the track, and it works in everyday life. You can go to the same coffee shop to do your work on your laptop every day, and that's consistency. You can do that with the mindset of being friendly and open and networking as your intention, and that's when you bump into someone in line who happens to be looking for someone with your skillset to work with on a huge project, and they've seen you working away everyday and are interested in you.

Consistency plus intention equals results.

SPRINT THROUGH YOUR SETBACKS JOURNAL PROMPTS

Grab a notebook or just jot your ideas down on these pages!

WRITE FUTURE YOU A LOVE LETTER

Write yourself a note for you to read before a tough thing, whether it's a test or a race. I like doing this a few days beforehand, including some motivational notes and quotes along with my goals that I've set for the day.

CREATE YOUR "RACE DAY SCHEDULE" FOR WHATEVER YOU'RE DOING!

You may have noticed in this chapter, we got granular about what a race day looks like. I spend a lot of time racing, so every time I have a race, I make sure my plan is written out and dialed in. What do you do normally? This could be work, school or racing. Take some time to write out every aspect of your ideal race/school/work day and the schedule that you follow, from wake up to bedtime. Get granular—writing this out helps you create smart routines and follow through with them because you can see the benefits you'll get!

SET A REMINDER

It's really important to take some time to write down thoughts after a big event. Make a reminder on your phone for after that race, presentation or test to just jot down a few notes about how it went. I like to make a few notes about what went well first, then add a few things that I want to work on for next time. Definitely prioritize getting some positives in there: it's tempting to go a little negative and list out every single thing that went wrong, but what went right is just as important!

TRUST

BOSTON UNIVERSITY LAST CHANCE MEET | MASSACHUSETTS, USA | 2022

"The only way we can make the most of our lives is to make the most of our moments. Today, wherever you are, decide to stay. We can know the gifts that lie in the present only if we stay in it long enough to receive them."
—Cleo Wade

Getting records on the track might sound like something that happens often. After all, there are so many specific events, there's indoor and outdoor track, and there are so many ways you can get a record: world record, national record, provincial record, school record, fastest time of the year… But here's the thing: it's still not easy. It's really, really difficult. (There's a reason my dad's World Record is still standing *decades* later!)

So, in 2022 when I got the 400 meter indoor record in Quebec, it was a big moment. And it definitely did not come easily… it also came a full six years after I got my school record, so you can see that it takes a lot of time between wins like that!

Beyond that one race, 2022 was a good year for me—and not just because of the results. It was a good year because it's when I finally relaxed into two major forms of trust: trusting myself, and trusting the process. Neither came naturally to me and at times, those two types of trust are in direct conflict with each other. You have to be able to trust the training process and listen to your coach and believe that slowly, you're going to see improvements in your run. But at the same time, you need to be able to listen to your body and know when there's something actually wrong. Feeling tired and a little fatigued is normal. Feeling aches and pains after a hard lifting session or a long practice on the track is normal. Feeling a nagging pain that won't go away, even if it's subtle enough that you can still run despite it? That's not normal, and you have to trust yourself enough to look into it instead of pretending it's not happening. If you just keep trusting the process and following your coach's plan despite developing a stress fracture, you're setting yourself back, not pushing yourself forward. It's a delicate balance.

So there we were, one year post-COVID. Most of us haven't had much of an indoor season since back in 2019, since so much was shut down and travel was so difficult for the last two years. I'd had one solid outdoor season since then, but it still felt like I was getting my feet back under me from all the disruptions when indoor season rolled around. It felt like such a huge relief to not have restrictions and testing protocols at every race. I understood why we needed them, of course, but they're really stressful! It was also right after the Olympic year where I didn't make the team, and it was just a really strange year for the Olympics in general. But suddenly, it was January of 2022, things were feeling normal again, and Paris 2024 wasn't too far away.

In fact, things were so normal that I was able to take a modeling job in early February out in Vancouver for lululemon, right in the middle of the season. I was training well and early racing had been going smoothly. Taking a job like that isn't ideal during race season, but then again, neither is being broke. Plus, this was a big shoot for lululemon! So, off I went.

It was a little hectic, since the timing meant that I would get back and have my first indoor race the day after I got home. But I told myself that this is a nice way to balance out my training and what I like to do outside of track for work. And it all worked out: the meet I'd come back for was at York University where I train in Toronto, so there were no surprises. The only downside was the timing, since the race had a 9AM start, which meant I had to get up super early because you have to warm up and be there at least two hours before. Not ideal when you just flew in from the West Coast! But the first race went well and I made it into the semifinals at 11AM, where I actually tied my indoor personal best. I was so proud of that. I even managed to nap in the afternoon before the finals, where I ran my second best time!

I remember thinking, 'Wow, you just had a big trip and still raced really well. Be proud of yourself and know that you can handle more than just track on your plate.' In a strange way, that combination of work followed by a race gave me such a boost of confidence. In the next couple of weeks, I was hitting really hard workouts while getting ready for a big meet in Massachusetts at Boston University. The meet was a chance for me to go for the World indoor qualification standard of 52.9 for the 400. I went in feeling confident because the training had been going well, I was super dialed in, and I was sticking to the plan.

Part of the plan was some in-race tactics that I needed to change. I normally wasn't a very aggressive racer. I ran hard, but I wasn't really playing the game and racing other people. My coach had given me a new focus: cut in first. Compared to outdoor track, indoor is so much more tactical. When you're outside, the turns are so much larger and you're just running in your own lane for the whole time. There's no cutting in, it's all about running your individual best. When you're racing indoors, you're running in your lane for 150 meters and then cutting into the inside lane. Then, you're running the last half of the race knowing someone's behind you. The thrill of it is honestly unreal.

Up until that point, I hadn't been taking the lead in races and I hadn't been cutting in first. I was more inclined to wait and finish strong, trying to come around other racers in the final moments.

Being more aggressive from the start and taking advantage of that first half of the race wasn't something I had ever focused on. On the indoor track, a 400 meter race is two laps. The first lap is 200 meters in your lane that you started in. But in the second half, you cut over to lane one. You can run in any lane, but in lane one, you're going have the best shot at winning. That's because you're technically running less if you cut into lane one first, because your competitors then need to come around you.

I try to set process-based goals for each race that I do. This definitely doesn't look like writing down that I'm going to set a personal best at each race. First of all, that's just impossible, and second, it's not really a process-based goal, something I can take action on other than by trying to run really fast. Plus, if you continually set goals that you can't actually hit, you just feel like crap every time you don't hit them.

In fact, if you constantly are setting any kind of in-race goals that you're not hitting, you actually end up a little desensitized to those goals because you sort of feel like writing them down is just going through the motions: you don't actually believe that result will happen.

Your race goal should be a piece of the racing puzzle that is going to make a big enough difference in the outcome that it will feel like a win if you make it happen. With a process goal like cutting in first, it isn't a guarantee that you'll win because some other girl may be faster. But if I did it, it was definitely going to change up the dynamic of the race. At that point, every race where I didn't cut in first, I didn't win. So it's pretty clear that cutting in first could change how the race plays out.

For me, having a goal like that was a big mindset shift. I could focus just on the cutting in, and there was a good chance that it would lead to a winning result. I know that my strength in the 400 is the second half of the race. So if I cut in first, that meant the first half of the race was taken care of and then I could do what I do best. A goal like that felt like I was finally working with myself as opposed to just playing by someone else's race plan.

When you don't cut in first, when you wait for somebody else to come in ahead of you, that's a big gamble if you're going for the win. You're anticipating the person ahead of you will slow down rather than you speeding up, which is such a strange tactic to me. You can't bet on someone going out super hard and then crumbling at the 300 meter mark at the elite level.

So at that race, I was determined to be the one to cut in first. It was my last chance to make the Indoor Worlds Team for Canada and I was up against some professional American runners, but I was confident. Running with other top pros has its advantages: Even if they beat you, you may run faster because you're running with them, which meant I was chasing both the win and the qualifying standard. I just knew I had to keep up with those girls.

The track was so busy when I got there. There were hundreds of people warming up for this meet: college kids, pro athletes, and so many spectators. Even in the warmup, you had to be so careful— you really had to stay in your own lane because there were people running past, and other races were happening simultaneously. It was wild. This is one of those races where you have to be super prepared. You need to be very, very on time. You have to know where to go, because they will start without you. So with that in mind, I got there more than two hours early so I would have extra time to warm up since it was so crowded and chaotic.

For World Indoor Track and Field, there are only six lanes versus the eight lanes you have outside. So they can only allow so many athletes and there are less events in general. In the 400, I knew the four other girls I was racing with had all been putting up some hot times, all in the 51s, so I was intimidated, but I also felt like today could be my day. My warm up felt good. But when I got to the line for check in, there was only one other girl there. The other girls didn't show up for the event! And all I could think was, 'Oh no. How am I supposed to cut in first when there's only one other person?' I knew this girl, too. I knew she was racing better than me. She was faster than me.

Deep breath. I told myself that regardless of how weird the situation was, I was going to stick to my plan and trust the process. Cut in first, and that's a really good sign. So I get in my blocks and it still feels so bizarre that we're the only two runners on the line. I usually prefer running on the outside so I have people chasing me the whole race, but with one other person, it's almost like you're running solo.

When you've been running for so many years, you learn to anticipate the gun going off. And when you get into your blocks, you end up creating some kind of mantra or a cue. For me, it's 'Push.' So I'm thinking that the whole time as I'm waiting to hear the starter pistol. I'm not thinking about the rest of the race, I'm just thinking 'push' so I can push out of the blocks with maximum force. I let a deep breath out when we're a few seconds from going. The deep breath out is really important because when I bring my hips up, press into those blocks with my heels and set my position a second or two from the start, I'm going to breathe in and then hold it until the gun goes. You have to be prepared to really sling-shot yourself out to have that good start. When you hear "set," everything goes blank because you know that in a matter of two seconds, you're about to go run as fast as you can in 52 seconds.

So when I breathe in, everything stops, time stops, and I just let my mind go. I'm just waiting for any noise to start running. That's why everyone needs to be quiet at the start: if someone yells in the crowd, most of the runners are going to be off and sprinting because we're so primed to go. I'm not listening for a gunshot, I'm listening for a sound. You're not trying to be analytical and think about what sound you hear, you just go when you hear anything.

The gun goes and we start running. And strangely, all I can hear is one person, despite the huge crowded stadium. I can hear my old teammate Mariam, who was there running the 60-meter hurdles. She's just screaming and cheering me on the entire time, because she's the only person who knew me personally at the meet!

When I pushed out of the blocks, I was running like it was a 60 meter race. I'd raced on this track before, the ground felt familiar and I was just in my zone. You don't always feel this confident and comfortable, but indoor track is nice because even if it's a new stadium you're in, you know what it's going to feel like. So here I am, I'm out and running what feels like a pace that's so much faster than what I usually can hold. But that's the whole point, pushing that early pace to cut in first. I'm feeling really strong, and I'm thinking, 'Oh my gosh, here it is, I'm going to cut in first.' I'm closing on the 180-meter mark and I'm there first. I can hear the other girl breathing down my neck, I slingshot myself down the track, and I cut in first.

Racing against just one person sounds easier, but mentally, it's harder when you think about doing the cut in first. I had to have the audacity to cut in first. That meant being confident enough to challenge her as a specific person, not just as someone in a pack of racers. And I knew she was coming into the race ranked faster than me. But I also think that was to my advantage: when I did cut in first, I think she may have assumed I would fade and she'd be able to come around me. But I know my finish is strong, so even though I figured that she would assume I would fade, I knew that I wouldn't. Once I got to the front, I locked in. That was the key for me: I was locked into that race. There wasn't a chance that I was going to let her pass me.

We hit the 200 meter mark and get the bell for the last lap and I'm running, running, running, just completely all out. I'm entirely in my zone, but I can feel the other girl so close to me. Now, everybody's screaming. But I still hear my friend. Through seeing red, I'm still thinking to myself, 'You're actually following the plan. This isn't as scary as I thought.' Because when you're doing it, there's nothing else but to do it.

I'm still running for all I'm worth, and I know she's closing. Her shoe grazes the back of my heel, but luckily, I keep my momentum and we don't both go down. It's just enough to let me know she's still right there. I don't have this yet. Thankfully, I don't panic, I just take more energy from that. I kept going and I crossed the finish line in first.

I looked over to my left and I saw the time and it was 52.668 seconds. I not only executed my plan, I won the race, I got the Quebec record, and I qualified for the Indoor World Championships in Serbia! Trust the process.

I could have let the plan go when it was just me and the one other girl on the line. It would have been easy to just assume that I would be finishing behind her, that I would have no hope of cutting in first. For some reason, it's easier to picture a race with several runners working out better than a race that's just you and one other girl. It's easier to get in your head when you know that your one competitor has faster times than you. To be able to block that out and still race according to plan—that wasn't easy, but it paid off.

That was the last chance for me to solidify my place on the Canadian team and to qualify as an individual, not just as someone on the relay team. I felt like I was getting not just my coach or the provincial coach's approval, I was stamping my own approval.

Indoor track is even weirder than outdoor track if you're new to the sport. When it comes to team selection for indoor season, the only real measurement the committee has to go off of is how well you are competing indoors—even if you're great outdoors, you need that indoor experience because it is different. Running the standard is really important. But because there are less events and less spots, Indoors is a very cutthroat team, and it's also a small team. In a way, it's more of a stepping stone to racing outdoors. It's not the be all and end all track team. But making that team did give me that reminder that I can make teams on the individual side.

The most fun part of the race was being able to watch it again on the broadcast. It was so funny because the announcer was saying, "She's off to a good start," but then immediately followed it with, "Will she be able to hold it?" I don't think anyone expected me to win—he definitely didn't!

Watching yourself race is difficult and kind of cringe-y, but it's also really important. It's the best way to catch mistakes. I used to just live in denial. If I didn't watch it, the mistake didn't happen. But now, I realize it's so important to watch it if you want to make progress: you can't improve what you don't understand. I needed to see me having less-than-ideal starts in races to really understand how they were impacting my finish. I watch the races now and try to watch myself almost as if I'm not me. I try to be totally objective and pretend I'm watching someone else. I try to think, 'If I was coaching that girl, what would I tell her?'

I no longer try to shy away from what I need to work on. I know it's all part of the process and because I've seen how much I improve when I do pay attention, I've been able to have less judgment and stop beating myself up when I watch those playbacks. Criticism about my run isn't criticism about me as a runner, it's just about one part of that race. I can look at a race and say, "I could have been more aggressive on the first 100. I could have been more intentional here." (I do also look for what went right, because that's also important. It's about finding that balance between critique and praise.)

And once that's done, it's about using that information in a constructive way. How are we going to make these changes? Is there something I can work on in practice? Is there a drill I need to add? Do I need to change my pre-race routine?

That day, nothing went exactly according to plan. It was a chaotic and hectic warmup. There was only one other girl in my race instead of five. She clipped my heel in the last stretch. Any of those factors could have changed the race. It was a reminder that at the end of the day, you just have to execute your plan and if you're prepared enough, you'll be able to do it no matter what the situation is.

The next month, it was so exciting to get an email ratifying my Quebec record. Now, I have this place in running history. And I think that that record is a good example of trusting the process rather than going for an outcome: my goal wasn't to get the record, my goal was to cut in first. I wasn't going into the race thinking, 'I'm going to break the Quebec record.' I was going into it thinking, 'I'm going to take the lead and command the race by cutting in first.' That was a tangible thing I could control myself. I can't really control the Quebec record and having that number in my head isn't very helpful. Sure, it might sound motivating, but it doesn't help you tactically in a race. You need your process goals to actually be things that you can do in the race, things that you can execute.

I realized that the key for me to race well is to actually have a plan, so no matter what happens around me, I can execute. In that race, I realized something else: you can run against people who on paper are faster than you. And you can win. You have to have this inner desire to win and to push yourself. You have to fight for yourself. It's not going to be easy, and it's not going to be a guarantee. But it's going to be possible.

Here's the thing, though. It's easy to buy into the idea of trusting the process, and you do need to be totally committed to it for it to work. But trusting the process doesn't mean that you stop refining and assessing how things are going, and making changes as you go on. It doesn't mean stagnating and staying stuck. There's still room for experimentation and adding things in.

I try my best to look back at training and races after a season and think about what went well, but also where I still need to improve. This can be tricky between indoor and outdoor season, compared to the bigger break in the fall/winter when outdoor seasons has ended and we have more time to build base, but I think it's important to constantly be assessing and tweaking. So after an indoor season, even if I only have a couple weeks before competing outdoors, I try to see it as a mini-reset. I look back and figure out if there's anything I need to add or subtract that would be beneficial for an outdoor season. You can't go wrong by constantly trying to fine tune your process. Yes, you trust the big picture. But you have to be able to make tiny course corrections.

It's harder now than it ever has been to trust your own process and progress. I've been doing this for almost a decade and I still find myself scrolling Instagram, seeing what other racers are doing for their workouts and I catch myself questioning what I'm doing. I can't stop myself from looking at what the 49-second 400-meter runners are doing. I see that they're doing some really different strength and plyometric work. So, do I need to incorporate that? Possibly—but I know I shouldn't just throw that in on top of what I'm doing. If I want to change up my training, it's not just a matter of adding extra plyometrics, I need to talk to my coach and get his opinion and think through how it fits with what I'm doing.

Getting inspired by other people can be really helpful, stressing out about how your training stacks up compared to theirs is definitely *not* helpful. If you constantly switch up your routine based on how you see other runners training on Instagram, suddenly, your schedule and whole training program makes no sense. You start veering off from your original plan, adding a whole extra day of weights because you saw somebody else lifting more. That's not really going to be productive, it's just going to make you more sore. But maybe you saw that the runner you're watching on Instagram is doing a different type of deadlift than what you normally do. Instead of adding a whole extra strength session, what if you talk to your coach about swapping from that regular deadlift to the Romanian deadlift the 49-second runner is doing?

I want to be very clear, though, that trusting the process does not mean following your coach blindly. You should trust your coach in general—and if you don't, you may need a new coach!—but you're also the one who knows your body better than anyone. You have to be willing to speak up for yourself if something feels like it's not working. You have to be willing to question the process your coach has laid out, and be open to that conversation.

In 2023, I had to figure out the balance of trusting myself while still trusting the process, and it's something I'm still working on. But for a few weeks in the fall after the season was over, I was feeling a lot of pain in my leg and I was really worried about it. My coach was well-meaning, but he basically told me not to worry about it, not to let it get me down. It was normal. Maybe it was stress related, or just a hormone thing. But I've been an athlete for 10 years. I knew it wasn't that simple.

After a few days of trying to pretend that everything was fine, I knew there was something wrong despite what my coach said. So I went to the doctor, and he almost instantly told me I needed to take four weeks off of running. I was a step away from a stress fracture. I could cross-train, but definitely not run.

And on one hand, I can validate myself and say, "Look, I wasn't being hysterical or dramatic." I can be proud that I stood up for myself when my coach told me I just needed to shift my mindset. On the other hand, I really wish he had been right, because obviously, it's not ideal to be injured this year. And I have no desire to tell my coach, "I told you so." He was just doing what he thought was right for me. However, I needed to be able to stand up for myself and do what I *knew* was right.

The balance between trusting yourself and being proved right, while also trusting the process, means that what I'm left with is the simple question: "I'm right. But now what?" And that's where the real work begins.

SPRINT THROUGH YOUR SETBACKS JOURNAL PROMPTS

Grab a notebook or just jot your ideas down on these pages!

HOW CAN YOU BE PREPARED?

I spend so much time preparing and visualizing for races, especially when I'm getting ready to try something new like cutting in first. Both mental and physical preparation are key to reaching your goals. Ask yourself:

- When was a time you prepared really well for a test, a meet, a competition, or a presentation?
- What did you do that made your preparation so good?
- How can you do that same kind of preparation in other aspects of your life?
- How can you set yourself up for success for an upcoming presentation or meet?

HOW DO YOU KNOW WHO TO TRUST?

In this chapter, I talked a lot about learning when to push back against what my coach was saying, but also when to listen to him knowing that he has my best interests at heart. That's not always easy to do! You probably have a coach or teacher or parent in your life who you don't always see eye to eye with.

When these situations come up, I try to ask myself a few questions:

1. Have I made my stance clear? (In my case, that was carefully explaining exactly how my injury was progressing and how running was making my leg feel.)
2. Have you had an honest dialogue about it with the person? (Have you very clearly stated what you feel is right for you and what your solution to the situation would be? I've realized sometimes when I was trying to

tell my coach something about how I was feeling, I wasn't really expressing how I wanted to fix the situation, I was just telling him what was wrong.)

3. If you're still not in agreement, is there some neutral third party you can go to for an opinion? (This could be the school nurse, a guidance counselor, another teacher, a parent, or a doctor.)

4. Has my coach/teacher/parent been right in the past? Are they usually correct in their assessments and it's only afterwards that you (painfully) admit that they were right? (This may not inform this situation exactly, but it might help you see that they might have a point.)

Of course, it's also important to note that if you feel uncomfortable or like you're in any physical or emotional danger, you should immediately seek help from a trusted adult!

TEST YOUR CONSPIRACY THEORY

If you've done all of that work and still feel like you and your coach/teacher/boss/parent aren't seeing eye-to-eye, test out the Conspiracy Theory. Write out what exactly that person is trying to do to you, what their ulterior motive is.

For me, that would have looked like "My coach is trying to sabotage my training by having me run while injured so I can't make the Olympic team." Writing that out and reading it makes me immediately see just how ridiculous that idea is—but deep down, that's what was going through my brain!

The key is writing it down on paper. Don't just think through this exercise, actually handwrite it and look at it. As soon as I see my Conspiracy Theory in writing, I instantly feel less like my coach is out to get me, and it's easy for me to see that he's just acting in the way he thinks is best for me. Knowing that makes it a lot easier to come to a win-win situation. (PS: This also works for when you're in a fight or disagreement with a friend!)

ASK YOURSELF: "I'M RIGHT, NOW WHAT?"

I come back to this question often, because it's so easy to focus on "winning" an argument rather than looking beyond it to figure out what your next action step should be. Bookmark this question for when you find yourself in a situation where yes, you were "right" in an argument, debate or disagreement with your coach/parent/teacher/friend. It's not always ideal to be proven right (like in my case, where I did have an injury that forced me to stop running). So, when and if you are right, what is the next step going to be?

BALANCE

WORLD ATHLETICS CHAMPIONSHIPS | OREGON, USA | 2022

"It's not the load that breaks you down; it's the way you carry it."
—*Lena Horne*

Picture this: it's Saturday night and you're out for a hill workout at the park. There's a chill in the air, but it's crisp and just right for running hard. Sure, it's the weekend and you could be out with your friends instead of shivering at the base of the hill as your coach gives you and the other runners your instructions, but you know you're exactly where you want to be.

You warm up in the fading light and by the time you're ready to start your hill repeats—three sets of three reps—the road is only lit by streetlights and people with headlamps.

The first interval starts. You begin to churn your way up the hill, and on the way up, a bike whizzes by you, so close you can feel the air move.

The next hill, a family with a bouncing dog on a leash and two kids are making their way down, taking up the whole road. You dodge them as you pant your way to the top.

The next rep, there's a dog off his leash who decides running with you seems like more fun. Another dog joins him, and you're trying to get up the hill with two over-excited pups running around you in circles. A group of bikes comes flying past. A gaggle of walkers strolls down the hill, spreading out across the road. You're coming up to the finish of the hill, dodging dogs, strollers, cyclists —just trying to stay focused on that finish line.

It's so bad that you just have to laugh.

But by the last rep, you finally have it dialed. You don't dodge the dogs or the cyclists—you stay tight to the side of the road, but you firmly own your space, looking straight ahead and not getting out of the way for anyone. They can go around you—you don't need to dodge them. You hold your line.

You have your best hill rep of the night.

I wanted to start this chapter on balance with this hill workout, because it was the perfect metaphor for how life can feel. You're just out there trying to do your best and focus on your goal, but there are all of these obstacles, hurdles, and interruptions that keep getting in your way. Some of them are external and you don't have a choice but to respond to them—hello, off-leash dogs!—but others, like trying to dodge a group of walkers who are more than capable of just tightening up and letting you pass? Dodging around them versus firmly holding your line is your choice.

Whether you're an athlete or not, you probably have this mentality or this vision of yourself doing everything, being a super-woman. And then you try to do everything—you really try!—but quickly, reality sets in that you only have so much time and energy, and you just can't do everything or give everything your full attention.

Being an athlete can give you a toxic mindset, unfortunately. Because we're told from an early age that hard work is what matters, that you need to push yourself in order to succeed, it's easy to push *too* hard. We believe to be our best selves, we need to push all the time. You never think, 'wow, I've come so far and accomplished so much,' you just look ahead and think of every-thing that you still need to do. It's so hard for us to take that pause, look back, and think, 'wow, I'm really good.' We're afraid that if we think that, we'll let ourselves relax and we'll stop working so hard. We'll stop accomplishing anything.

That mentality is why so many of us—even young athletes in high school—push ourselves to do it all, to be everything to everyone. We never want to settle, we never want to admit that we can't or shouldn't be doing that one more thing.

Balance isn't about finding the perfect way to juggle all of the things—it's about figuring out what's the top priority in your life *right now* and focusing on that as much as possible. You'll have to do some stuff that isn't necessarily working towards that goal (more on that in a second) but a lot of the time, we add way more because we think we should... or because we're scared of going all in on our biggest goals.

If you want to achieve a lot as an athlete—or at school or in your career—you have to be all in. You can't keep adding things to your schedule and expect that you can do everything. When you try to do that, you may end up getting everything done, but it won't be done to your high standards.

Of course, the answer is not as simple as 'I quit my job and went all in on focusing on my training.' I still have rent to pay, and even when I am getting funding as a Canadian athlete, that still doesn't cover everything on a monthly basis—and carding comes and goes depending on how that past season has gone, so it's not reliable. Plus, there are also asks from sponsors and from different sports organizations, and those are important to me as well. Now, I approach all of them with a bit more care than I used to. I still say yes, but I make sure that it's on my own terms.

In 2022, I upset my balance—hard. In the last chapter, I talked about feeling like I didn't belong and like I had to earn my place on the track. I let that feeling dictate a few choices I made in early 2022, and it definitely caught up with me.

THEN:

February 20, 2022
7 am Wake up, check email
7:30 am Breakfast, get ready for track
8:15 am Bus to track
9 am 300+100m x 2 Special endurance practice session (2.5 hr)
11:30 am Bus home
12 pm Lunch, shower
12:30 pm Shoot, edit and write copy for 20+ videos to send to potential new clients for work
4 pm Lift weights (90 min)
6 pm Treatment
7 pm Dinner
8 pm Stretch and prepare for tomorrow's workout
9 pm Few more emails, finish copy
11:30 pm Bedtime — take a while to get to sleep since I shut my work down and went immediately to bed. Brain wouldn't stop buzzing!

This has always been me: I had a part time job when I was in high school, I was on the cross country team and the track team, I was an honor roll student, I loved taking extra language classes. Even back then, I felt like I had to do it all in order to be the best. But it was impossible then, and it's impossible now.

Flash forward to 2022, when I started a job that was technically part time but was essentially full time. It was at the same time we were leading up to Worlds and the Commonwealth Games, and when I took the job, it was only a few weeks after I'd finally gotten my carding—the government funding that helps elite athletes—back for the year.

In short, it was probably the *worst* possible time to take on a new job.

By the time we headed to Europe for the first time that season, I was already feeling the stress of balancing the two full-time jobs and quickly realized that yes, there are plenty of athletes who do some work on the side, or even have full-time jobs. But none of them were here racing. It was just me getting up to sneak in work before breakfast and training. The other athletes there knew that they needed to focus all of their attention on their one job: being an elite runner.

So, why would I sign up for a job like this in the first place? It's a good question. At the time, it felt like I wanted to have a bit more compartmentalization for my athletic career. In retrospect, I think it was because I knew what it was like to have carding taken away, so even when I got it back, I wasn't comfortable relying on it.

At the beginning, it seemed like the perfect gig: a part-time position in sales and social media with a small tech-based Canadian startup that was led by some great people. I wanted as much financial stability as I could possibly have—having had a lean year in 2021—and I thought 20 hours per week in the offseason and 10 hours in the racing season would be absolutely do-able. And the people at the startup not only understood my training and racing, they were excited to have me on board.

If you've ever worked at a startup, you're probably rolling your eyes reading that, and rightly so. 20 hours is never just 20 hours when you're in a new company where everyone is doing a bit of everything. It was off to the races as soon as I got hired, because they were looking for a partnership manager. I came in assuming that it would be some outreach and some social media, but I found out very quickly that it would be much more than that. And the flexible hours were less flexible than I assumed they would be. If you were in the right time zone, they weren't too bad, but if you were anywhere else in the world... nope.

Just a couple weeks after I started, I went to a training camp in

January of 2022 in Halifax, Nova Scotia. We would start training early, but even getting back from training by the early afternoon wasn't working out with work because I'd come back to dozens of messages from my boss. It quickly became clear that flexibility still meant getting things done on their schedule—I could just get up earlier to do it.

This wasn't their fault: I took on way too much when I was going to training camp for two weeks right after I got a new job. Opportunities like either of these can be hard to turn down, but if you say yes to everything, you're not going to be able to excel at anything. It's easy to try to blame other people, but at the end of the day, I made this schedule and these commitments.

So I started off on the wrong foot at work. By the time I got back from that camp, I felt even more underwater than when I started: I assumed there was an onboarding process where I would be taught all of the different programs we were using and have some mentorship for my new role, but it was really more learn-as-you-go, a situation where I wasn't just doing the work, I was also learning the software and programs I was supposed to be using. It's no surprise that it was very stressful trying to get up to speed with that while literally trying to get up to speed on the track.

I thought when I got home from camp that things were starting to calm down: I had two weeks where I was able to be on their schedule and it seemed smooth. But then I started competing in indoor track season.

It didn't go well—on either level.

Yes, my new boss had said they would happily support my Olympic goals. I think they really believed that. But until you're in this world, you don't really know what that looks like. Every company has their own goals and I had my own. That's a conflict. At the end of the day, the company is going to be my boss's priority, not my racing. And when it comes to deadlines in a small company, it's obvious who's not meeting those deadlines because there are only a few people who are working.

My running was still going well, but from week to week, my performance at the start-up felt like it was on a rollercoaster. One week it was a huge mess, the next, I'd feel like I was caught up. The stress from that became this kind of overflow in my workouts as time went on and I felt I wasn't really doing my best in either.

It all came to a head when I made the World Championship team that summer. I emailed my boss saying, "I'm not going to be able to work the 20 hours. I need to go down to the 10 we talked about when I'm traveling." I was met with the response, "Yes, no problem."

The problem was, they still expected the same amount of work to get done... in half the time.

I really pride myself in doing my work well and learning on the fly. But my willingness and excitement about learning is what got me in trouble: as I was trying to drop to 10 hours of work each week, the company got this new software that would send customized videos to prospective clients. So first, I had to learn this entirely new program. Okay, no problem. It took extra time, but sure, I can do that. I figured once I learned it, 10 hours would be fine. However, the point of the new software was that the videos we were making were personalized, which meant I needed to record them individually—which meant finding a quiet place to record, no matter where I was. The videos themselves were short—just one minute—but making them, I quickly realized, took about 30 minutes per video.

In the couple weeks I was traveling, I was working more than my 20 hours to figure all of this out, sneaking into closets and wherever I could find quiet spots to record 60 of these videos. While other athletes were lying on the couch or in bed with their legs up, foam rolling while watching reality TV to relax or Face-Timing with friends at home, I was literally hiding in a closet trying to speak quietly but clearly into a microphone to record the videos that I needed to get turned in. Even as everyone else went to bed early, I stayed hidden in the closet to get the project finished in time.

I went to bed hours later than everyone else, completely drained and exhausted, but with the project turned in on time... only to wake up to an email that the company dropped the project almost immediately because the videos weren't garnering new leads. There I was, doing all this extra work for this company to stay ahead and they weren't going to use the videos!

I just remember thinking, 'This might be the final straw.' I was meant to be working super part time, but it kept turning into full-time. This startup was still in an experimental phase, and I can't be in that experimental phase when I'm training and racing at the highest level. I'd had enough. This wasn't working out. But now, I just needed to figure out how to make that change. It's hard giving up something that you know is helping pay the bills, even when you know it's the right thing to do if you want the big payoff later.

Fast forward a week: We're in Portland for worlds, I'm about to head to the Commonwealth Games in a couple of days, so a major time zone shift is about to happen, which I know is going to make work even more disrupted... and on top of that, I'm trying to have my best performances, knowing that these meets are important heading towards the 2024 Olympics.

I can feel that I need to leave, and I can also tell that my boss, as supportive as she wants to be, is struggling with how much I'm able to contribute to the start-up. We're heading in different directions, but neither of us wants to be the one to say it.

Looking back, I should have just spoken up. It would have saved us both a lot of time and stress, but when you're in it, you're so focused on just getting everything done that you don't pause to really reflect on what needs to happen in the long term.

But finally, with the Commonwealth Games looming, I knew we needed to part ways, and we were able to make that clean break without any major blowups. It was awkward and uncomfortable, and I felt a little like I was letting them down and letting myself down, but I knew it was the right thing to do.

The first day I woke up with no work for the start-up on the schedule, I had this sinking feeling that I was right back to where I had started not even a year before. No extra work coming in, just training to focus on. And that was terrifying. But more than that, I felt free and focused for the first time in months.

Track was once again my priority—the way it should have been all along.

NOW:

November 10, 2023
8 am Have breakfast + write in journal what I'm grateful for and intention for the day
11 am Training session
1 pm Lunch
1:30 pm Lift Session
3:30 pm Decompress at home
5 pm Commute to Culture Running Event
6 pm Speak at Culture Running Event
7 pm Eat dinner provided at running event
8 pm Commute home
9 pm Wind down
10 pm Bedtime

When I look back at that part of my life, I realize that I thought that in order to be taken seriously, I needed to be doing so much, all the time. But it's actually the opposite. The more I can have time to think clearly, to meet all the expectations I have for myself, the better I function. But as soon as I fall short on one thing, everything is derailed.

Now, I'm trying to find the optimal balance between being an athlete—that's the top priority, always—while making time for work that's aligned with the life I want to be living. It's still busy, but now, it's on my terms.

Yes, at the beginning when I took the job at the start up, I was really clear about my athletic goals and not being able to work more than 20 hours, but as I got into it and it became obvious that it was a full time job, instead of setting my boundaries more firmly, I just started trying to meet their expectations while also trying to meet my coach's expectations for me on the track.

I wanted to do all the work and the training because I wanted to show to myself—and everyone around me—that I was a capable athlete who could work and do it all. It was all about validation, even though at the time, I was trying to convince myself it was all about needing the money. It was that too, but it was just as much about validation.

That was a big wake up call.

And even now, writing about it, I struggle to share this because I know just how privileged it is to be able to focus on my career as an athlete instead of balancing working full-time and being an athlete. It almost makes me feel guilty because I know that there are athletes who don't have that choice. But at the same time, when I was trying to do everything, I realized that my mental health was deteriorating: I was anxious and stressed all the time. I was lucky that I was able to put my mental health above money.

After I left that job, I was able to go into the next year with a lot less stress, despite having less money in the bank. And it made me think more laterally: I realized there were ways I could work that worked with my track schedule and actually enhance it. I'm much more flexible and still have a little bit of side income from things like speaking, personal sponsorships and modeling.

Instead of banking as much as possible right now, my goal has shifted to keeping my life as flexible as possible. Not feeling as though I have to prove that I can do it all has really been a game changer for my mental health.

I have all of my life to work. Right now, I need to remember that I'm in my prime for track and as I'm training six days a week, I can't work a full-time or rigid part-time job. Neither my training nor my work can flourish like that. As it is, I can actually look forward to training six days a week. I can show up and perform the way my coach expects me to.

But I wouldn't trade that season of work for anything: I found out a lot more about myself and actually started questioning why

I'm doing the things that I'm doing. Before that, I was on autopilot, just rolling through things, doing what seemed like a good idea at the time. Now, I know that I don't have to put *everything* on my plate. I can pick and choose when I do so.

I've also realized that you're never fully in balance and there are always opportunities and obstacles that can easily throw you out of balance. I noticed right away after I stopped working that job that suddenly, with my newfound free time, I had the urge to fill it. But being balanced doesn't mean being constantly busy. Having breathing room doesn't mean it should be filled. I realized I have this tendency when things are going really well—like when I had finally gotten carded again and track was going great—to believe that I can and should pile more and more on. But really, what I should be thinking is, 'This is a good place to be.'

It goes deeper than just feeling like, 'Okay, I have time, I should add more work,' though. Looking back, I can see my younger self and understand that my decision to take that job right when things were going well for me in running wasn't just a financial decision or a scheduling decision—it was so deeply rooted in fear.

I felt like, 'I just got a second chance at carding, but I don't know how long this will last,' because I remembered that stress of having it taken away and *not* having it. So if the year didn't go well, at least I would still have my job. It also gave me both this weird sense of pride—that I can work and be a carded athlete—and an excuse, because now I was a carded athlete, but one who was still working, so if anything wasn't going well, I had a built-in reason. That's just setting yourself up for failure.

Being an athlete as a full-time job is a very, very weird life. Our job doesn't end at 5PM—we're always on the clock. Every part of our life translates into how well we can do our jobs. It's unconventional and it's hard to understand even as an athlete. On one hand, it's all so natural to us that it often doesn't feel like work, it feels like it's what we're meant to do. But on the other hand, to excel in a sport where milliseconds count, everything—your training, your sleep, your nutrition, your mental health—has to be so dialed in that if you go slightly off the plan, it can put your job security in danger.

From the outside, it might look like a hugely privileged place to be. But just because it's an unconventional format of producing value, that doesn't mean that it's not *work*. I train six days a week and that's just the beginning. You aren't always making enough money to survive—you're not guaranteed minimum wage as an athlete!—and there's no real job security, especially at this level. That means even though it's impossible to do this while holding down a full-time job, you still need to find a way to make money outside of *just* running.

I knew when I left that job that I would need to find some other way to make money—but I also knew it would have to be on my terms. I needed to find a balance of work that would let me stay focused on my Olympic goals, which meant looking for work that was flexible and less structured, so my training would always be the primary focus.

That meant shifting my narrative from, 'I want to be taken seriously, and I'll do everything and anything so people can know that I'm running while I'm working because I'm just this good.' But if the goal is to make it to the Olympics, to be the best that I can be at my event, that doesn't align with working for someone else's dream. That idea of needing to prove myself by keeping a full-time job on top of running doesn't align.

It's an easy decision—sort of. What a lot of books like this forget to mention is just how hard it is to pursue a running career when you're not bringing in a steady paycheck from another job. I was lucky that I was able to shift to part-time work and still be able to afford basics, but it meant getting frugal and not spending money on any of the extras.

Endurance sports like running, cycling and triathlon, or any individual sport, can be really challenging when it comes to defining what it means to be a pro or elite athlete. It's hard to feel like you're fulfilling your "duty" as a pro. You never know exactly where the line is as far as what makes you a pro and that can make you constantly question your identity and what you're trying to balance in the first place. It's not like a team sport like football or hockey where you get drafted, you're on a team and getting paid, and that's when you're a pro. In running, almost all of us have to figure out secondary careers or other pieces to the puzzle in order to make a living, all while still trying to train and race professionally.

It's stressful, especially at first when those regular paychecks stopped coming in, but the freedom to train the way I needed to be training, just focusing on what was going to get me to the next level, was worth it.

Of course, that doesn't mean I just ran and trained. Even at the highest level, there's a lot more to being a pro athlete. But now, it was happening on my terms, and I was being thoughtful about everything that went on my calendar. For example, in 2023, I did a lot more public speaking. One event happened on a Thursday night, which meant that it would be directly following a track practice with my training group and I didn't want to miss that. Micha from 2022 would have just said yes to both without any prep or planning, and would have been quite literally sprinting between the two since one finished at 5:30 and the other began at 6, I'd need to change in between and find time to maybe eat something. Not this time. I let the people organizing the talk know I'd be a bit late and asked about the dinner situation and when I'd be able to eat, since the event did include a dinner. I also asked about if I'd be able to get changed there and exactly what they needed from me in terms of speaking, so I could be prepared.

I would have been nervous about asking questions like that in the past because I would have been afraid to seem like I was asking for too much, but now I know that no one minds me asking for clarification—if anything, that makes me seem more prepared and ready for the talk! In this case, the dinner would be after the talk, so I knew to bring a protein shake to drink on the way to the event after my workout, and I would be able to quickly change my clothes when I got there.

Having that information ahead of time really made the whole talk much smoother and much more rewarding and fun for me. I got to meet a lot of people, including sponsors, and I didn't feel stressed (or hungry) the entire time. I got to chat with a lot of new runners and give them some hopefully helpful advice, and I wasn't feeling burned out or exhausted. And even though it was a night-time event, I was still home and in bed at a reasonable hour... which was good, because we had an early big workout on Friday!

Hopefully what's come across so far is that being a pro athlete may look glamorous and even seem easy from the outside. But now, you and I both know that's not the case. There's such a fine line that I try to walk now between training and work, especially in seasons where I don't have funding, which can come and go based on your recent performances. I'm always careful with my spending: I live in a one-bedroom apartment with my partner, we cook most of our meals at home, and we don't take on any major expenses. Heading into 2024, I didn't have funding because of my injuries that kept me out of doing some of the key races and not performing at my best in the middle of the season. It's frustrating, especially since I ended the season in really good form, but I came into that form after the decisions for carding were already made—and I was only one spot away from getting it. That's hard to handle, and it's hard to see the positive in being off of the carding list. It means not just trying to get better and faster to make it for next year, and to be pushing to be on the Olympic team without all the governmental resources some of the other athletes have access to, but also spending time reaching out to potential sponsors and looking for different athlete grants from the federal and provincial government. People think athletes just run, but we also spend so much time hustling to get sponsors, and then working hard to keep those sponsors! But when you're not carded, it really forces you to focus and puts you in this position to decide that you're going all in.

So, how do you keep going, in a balanced way that's still sustainable for you? I think a lot of you reading this probably struggle with this question. If you're an athlete, you may not getting paid a big salary to race or compete (yet!). Maybe you're still in school and you know you need to keep your grades up while fully committing to doing well at Nationals for the track team, and you're struggling to juggle homework and practice but you don't have a choice. Maybe you're working full-time and trying to qualify for the Boston Marathon, and you're having a hard time getting your key workouts in but you can't just stop working on that report due to your boss next week. We all have seasons where finding balance can be really challenging—and the times you do find it, it's not likely going to stay that way.

The first step, I think, is to stop putting blame on other people and carrying a lot of resentment towards them or towards your situation. In 2022, I spent so much energy being annoyed at the work that I had on my plate, rather than trying to be calm and figure out a solution. I accepted it as something that was going to make me mad and tired and wasted a lot of emotional energy. When I found out I wasn't getting carded for 2024, I tried to not be in that same place of resentment, especially since with carding, one year you can get it and be on top of the world and the next year, it's gone—it's a roller coaster if you're not careful about managing your emotions. If I let the decisions from other people control how I feel, I'm giving my power to them. And that's not their responsibility. With carding, they're not there to decide whether I'm ready for the Olympics or not. They're just there to decide who gets funding—that's it.

Once you can stop feeling that sense of resentment and blame, you can look more rationally at a situation and figure out what your next best step is. If you're struggling with practice and school, stop being mad at your math teacher for assigning you too much homework, and instead, maybe you could have a talk with her about getting an extension or getting a tutor to help you once a week so you don't keep struggling. That's much more useful than just sitting there with your math textbook and hating your teacher.

The second step is seeing the positive and the opportunity in things. I look at not having carding as a push for me to fully commit to being an athlete. If I really want it, now I have to fight for it. It means going into the next season with a lot more clarity as to what I need in order to make it. I need to run faster. It's very simple. So how do I get there? I believe in my abilities. If money is the only factor that's holding me back or causing me stress, how can I figure that out? It turns out you often have a lot more resources than you realize and a lot more people that can support you.

The same applies when I feel annoyed or stressed about a request to do something like a talk for a sponsor or for some running event put on by Athletics Canada or one of the other government sports groups. It's easy to get grumpy about having to do a speaking engagement because it does take away from training, eating and recovering on your normal schedule. But if you look at it like that, you're right back to feeling resentment. Instead, I think about the fact that there's so much opportunity in those events. You never know who you'll meet or who you'll influence or help with something you say.

The third piece is being confident in yourself and your abilities —and not assuming you know what other people are thinking. With carding, it's remembering that just because I didn't get carded one year doesn't mean that the coach doesn't think I'm talented or the governing body doesn't think I'm going to make it. They're not thinking about me like that, only I'm thinking about it like that! For you, maybe you're feeling like your math teacher thinks you're not smart, and that's why you're afraid to ask her for the extension or for extra help, even though you're really struggling. Being confident doesn't always mean thinking that you're super smart, though: It can also mean being confident enough in yourself to ask for help. (And your teacher doesn't think you're dumb, I promise!)

Something doesn't go as well as you hoped it would? Instead of looking at it as a failure, what if you look at it as an experience that taught you something for next time? Every time I do a talk or give a speech, I think of a bunch of ways I could have improved—but instead of being mad at myself or thinking I'm a terrible speaker, I make notes and use that information for the next time.

As an athlete, you have to be okay with adapting, because you're always going to be navigating changes in your training, working on something new, honing a weakness, or dealing with an illness or injury. If you're not adaptable, you won't get very far.

Your fourth step is to realize that what you're doing is enough, and to stop comparing yourself and your schedule to what everyone else is doing. It does take a while to really convince yourself of this. I think a lot of times, as women especially, we don't feel we're ever enough. So when I first gave up that full-time steady job, I had constant chatter in my head telling me I wasn't doing enough.

That's how a lot of runners end up burned out or injured or overtrained: we think we need to do more, more, more to fill the time that we do have. But in an individual sport like track, it's so easy to overdo it. Unlike sports like football or hockey with defined practice and training, training for track is so individual. Some people can train for 30 hours every week and be at their best, others will be at their best with 18 hours of training. Some athletes need to sleep 11 hours every night, some feel great after eight.

Fifth, it's time to take yourself seriously. This is about confidence again, but it really means having confidence to balance *your* life for *your* goals. To get to where I'm making a living as a pro means that I have to act as though I am already a pro athlete, and pro athletes know what their bodies need in order to excel. I can't be second-guessing myself all the time. I can't be adding things on my plate that have nothing to do with my ultimate goals. I have to take myself seriously.

And I'm the only one who can do that. I realized that when I was working full-time in another job, and when I struggle to take myself seriously as an athlete, I have this concept that "they" don't see me as a real athlete. But who are "they" really? *No one.* No one is thinking about me as much as I am. Is there someone actually out there trying to stop me from running, or saying they don't think I'm a real athlete? No. There is not a person whose only job is to keep me from my goals.

Finally, balance is found when you realize that it's never going to be perfect. Balance isn't about the perfectly organized schedule. Balance is about having a well-thought out schedule and some parameters on your time, yes, but it's also about being flexible and open to seeing opportunities when they come.

The reality of being a high-performance athlete is that we've trained ourselves to get through tough workouts and races, even when they're uncomfortable or unpleasant. That translates to being able to do the same in other parts of our lives. I know that on Thursday I have a practice in the afternoon, and I just got the call that I won't have carding for the next year, but I still have a call with a sponsor and a talk that evening. I can handle it. I'll still show up and be the positive, optimistic person I am for the talk. It's not going to be comfortable. I am going to be feeling some feelings about it. But because I've pushed myself on the track, I know just how strong I can be.

SPRINT THROUGH YOUR SETBACKS JOURNAL PROMPTS

Grab a notebook or just jot your ideas down on these pages!

GET CLEAR ABOUT YOUR GOALS

Let's start with a few questions to help you hone on what your actual goals are!

- What is your top priority in your life right now? (And yes, of course you'll want to write down more than one... but try to keep it to three, maximum.)
- How much time are you giving your main priority?
- In an ideal week, how would you be going after your goal? What can you add that would be helpful? (For a track runner, adding extra recovery sessions might be a great one that's often ignored!)
- In an ideal *day*, how would you be going after your goal? What are the tiny things you could do on a daily basis? For example, if you're serious about being a track athlete, things like making time to stretch or hydrate enough are really important but often overlooked!

GET HONEST ABOUT YOUR CURRENT SCHEDULE

Now that you know what you want to make time for, it's time to look at where you're currently spending your time.

- Look at your last couple weeks on your calendar—are you actually giving your main goals as much time as you think? Or are there other things that keep getting in the way?
- When you write out your daily schedule or to-do list, can you actually get it all done? What usually gets skipped or moved to next week?

- Are there any things you're doing regularly that you could easily drop off of your schedule that would allow you more time and energy to focus on your main goal? (Obviously things like homework or a job you need in order to pay rent aren't going to be negotiable, but maybe it's time to give up that spot on student council if you really want to be focused on your volunteer work!)
- Where are you holding onto a resentment or a lack of confidence that could actually be holding you back instead of helping you? Is someone making you feel like you 'have' to be doing something? If so, do they honestly feel that way, or are you just projecting? (This is especially true with parents—we think they want us doing a million things, but most of the time, it's in our heads... see the last chapter's prompt about Conspiracy Theories!)

WRITE OUT AN IDEAL SCHEDULE BASED ON YOUR GOALS AND CURRENT LIFE

Whether you use a paper planner or a digital one, take some time to draft a new weekly schedule that leaves you time to focus on your goals, without neglecting or ignoring the other 'must do' pieces of your life. While you won't be able to hit this schedule every week, having it to refer back to is a good reminder of how you can make space for your goals.

BELONGING

"Never limit yourself because of others' limited imagination; never limit others because of your own limited imagination."
    —Dr. Mae Jemison

I was born in Montreal, Quebec, a French-speaking city in Canada. For my whole early childhood, I spoke French, watched French TV shows and read French books. At least, I did until my mom got a job opportunity in Atlanta, Georgia, on CNN. That meant at six years old, I would be moving there with her, leaving behind my grandmother, my friends, and my entire culture.

I remember vividly being so afraid to speak English because I knew I had an accent that would stand out from Americans, especially from a southern American accent. And while I spoke and understood English, French was my first language and I was much more comfortable speaking in it.

When we first moved there, my mom put together a playdate for me and her co-worker's daughter. The playdate was going well... at least, it was until I couldn't remember a specific word in

106

English and my French spilled out. The girl said to me in an accusatory tone, "Why don't you speak *American*?"

At the time I didn't have enough life experience to retort that English is my second language and that American isn't a language, but that's besides the point. I was so embarrassed by my accent and worried about coming across as less intelligent. I immediately felt like I was an outsider.

I guess I've been hard on myself since I was six years old. Even then, I didn't feel like I belonged, and that was a feeling that would continue throughout my life.

What I've learned is that there is no finish line with belonging. There is no external cue that will make you feel like you belong if you don't believe it. Belonging doesn't come from setting records, winning races, or even from being part of a team. Yes, that's part of it—but belonging can't come from the outside. If you're always striving for something, whether it's the spot on the squad or the next promotion at work, and you think that once you get there, you'll finally feel like you belong, I hate to be the one to break it to you, but once you get there, you still won't really feel like you made it. The outside accomplishments do help, and they do give you external validation. These things matter, especially when it comes to actually making a living in the sport—but they only take you so far, and they're not going to get you through the hard times. Truly feeling like you belong? It turns out it's an inside job.

You might think that because of my mom and dad, I would immediately feel like I belonged at the track. It's my legacy, right? While that can be motivating, it can also feel like it's a crushing set of expectations and standards that are impossible to live up to. For me, feeling like I didn't belong was even more pronounced because of who my parents are: it feels like if you do belong, you only belong because of who they are, not who you are. When your mom and your dad are record-holders, Olympians, legends in the sport, you hear about it. A lot. You meet a new coach or a journalist, and the first thing they tell you is how they saw your mom at a race, or interviewed her at some point. It's not intentional, but it makes you feel like you have a lot to live up to, and you're not doing it.

Belonging at the track can also be very black-and-white: in a lot of ways, you're either in or you're out as an elite athlete. In Canada, when you get carded as an athlete, it doesn't mean you're showing ID to get into a club... Well, it sort of does. But not *that* kind of club. Being carded means that Athletics Canada has made you eligible for government funding so you can afford to live and train. It also gives you access to the track where the Olympians train and practice, as well as services for athletes, like physical therapy. For a young track athlete, carding allows you to chase your dreams. And it signals to the rest of the world that you're a professional athlete who deserves to be here.

I lost my carding for the first time in my career in 2019. That meant my access to the indoor track where we all trained was cut off—like someone took my license and cut it up. I felt like the people who were carded and the people who were considered a part of the national team were more elite. And in a lot of ways, they were. When you don't have carding, you immediately stop being a priority, and that makes you start to question what you're doing here in the first place.

When they didn't give me credit, I stopped giving myself credit.

Going from carding to no carding is like getting kicked out of first class and stuck in economy mid-flight. To even get into the indoor track at the Athletic Hub at York University to practice, I felt like I was sneaking in: if you're not a carded athlete, you can only get in if you're a training partner of a carded athlete... and then, you can only go in if you're with that athlete. The day before I lost carding, I could walk through that door without question. I was a welcome member, I was part of the club. The next day, that was gone.

To say it feels like a barrier is an understatement. Every time you walk in, you feel like you don't really belong because you know you're only allowed in because of someone else. You still have some access to things like physical therapy, but you know you're at the bottom of the list and if a carded athlete needs treatment, your appointment gets bumped. This sort-of inclusion makes you feel like you're not enough—and the reminders are constant.

You feel uncomfortable. There's this constant voice saying, 'I'm only here because I'm my training partner's training partner.'

Looking back, I think that not getting carded made me want to be a better athlete and focus on what I needed to strengthen. At the time, it just hurt.

I had hoped that 2020 would be the year I would get my carding back and I'd get back on track to make it to the Olympics that same year. We all know how that went. For athletes like me, the pandemic was even more of a problem from a professional standpoint, because carding was frozen: there was no way to get carded, no matter how good my times were.

It should have been a disaster—but the frustration and the lack of racing translated to something different: focus. Without the pressure to race and perform, I actually had time to develop and get consistent. With the opportunity to belong to a team or to belong by winning a race suddenly off the table, I didn't have any of those external metrics to rely on to feel like a real athlete. I just had myself and what I could do day after day. It took a year, but when everything shut down and there wasn't access to anything for anyone, something in me finally switched.

I had to say to myself, 'Okay, I'm not carded. So, now what?' Now, I have more time to focus on what I need to focus on because I don't have to check in with Athletics Canada and the national coach. I don't have to send in my training plans and let them know what I'm doing. They don't care, and there's freedom in that. Before, I had felt like I had to constantly prove that I could be good, and that wasted time and energy. I had a lot of anger about the situation. I had a lot of discomfort being at the track. I wanted to show them. But I realized that wasn't the point. It never was.

I was always good, but I had to believe it. I started to.

When 2021 came around, I had found my rhythm again and I was racing more consistently. I got my carding back... but when the Olympic nominations finally happened, I didn't make the team. I found out at the track when other people were getting nominated that I wouldn't be going.

I kept running.

Two weeks later, I finished off the season with a personal best in the 200 meter and my season's best in the 400 meter. I didn't have the Olympics, but I had the carding again and that was enough to keep me going. But I still felt like I was on the outside, looking in. I was finally back on the National Team, but I still felt like my ID wouldn't work to get me into the Hub to train.

Early in 2022, I was nominated to be on the relay team for Worlds in Oregon. But at that point, I was still flashing back to not being selected the year before. There was a part of me that kept whispering, 'I don't even know if they're going to choose me. I don't know if they *should* choose me.' I had a run-off with another girl to see who was going to be in that fourth position for the relay, and I won. This was my chance to prove that I was ready to go and that they made the right decision. And I was terrified.

That terror translated into one of the worst races of my life in the relay. I was the only one at Worlds who hadn't run an individual race event, so I was going in very fresh. That sounds like a good thing, but it's not always the best position to be in. I had a great start to the race, but I was running backwards in the final stretch. I've never split so low. It felt like I didn't know where I was, I couldn't control my pace. I felt like even though my running had improved, my racing was still coming up short.

I thought the season was over, that I was going to be back to the drawing board trying to figure out how to come back next year. But then—while I was still in my hotel in Portland, Oregon, after that bad result at Worlds, getting ready to pack it up and go home—I got a call from Glenroy Gilbert, the head coach of Team Canada, asking if I wanted to run at the upcoming Commonwealth Games in England. He said I could run the 400 meter and the 4-by-400 relay as part of Team Canada.

I was getting a second chance. But there wasn't much time to celebrate it, or to be scared by it. We flew from Portland, Oregon, to Birmingham, England, a couple of days later. This was still COVID times, so not only did we have a 10 hour flight and a nine hour time change, we had to do COVID tests in the airport and then wait for our results for a couple hours before we were allowed to leave. To be honest, I didn't even know what was really happening by that point. It was a blur. But I knew 'I'm in Birmingham, we made it.' We were all in individual rooms just to make sure the team avoided a COVID outbreak, since obviously we'd all be self-contained. But we could spend time together outside and I invited a few people I knew from the team to sit outside in this great little garden spot and have tea. It took our minds off of running.

I went into my first 400 meter race at the Commonwealth Games still jet-lagged but made it through. I made it to the semis, but didn't make it further than that. However, there was still the team relay coming up in two days, so I was still hopeful.

The coach gave me a whole day off to recover and I actually ended up having some time with my former teammate, Aiyanna, and we found a great place where we got to just relax and talk about goals. For the first time in a long time, I felt like I was really able to connect with somebody who was in the same position as me. It hit me that I'm not going through this by myself.

The day of the team relay, I woke up feeling strangely calm. I attribute that to going to that botanical garden with my teammates, and just doing things outside of the track, having those conversations.

But at the track, the nerves started again. The thing with this team relay is that the coach had brought five runners but only four of us would have the chance to run. The start list and the starting order is decided at the last minute—it was a flashback to the Rio Olympics for me. And although that's frustrating, it makes sense: they want everybody to be ready so that you don't tune out. So I get there, we're doing our warmup, and halfway through, they stop us and sit us down to tell us the order for the race.

The first runner was going to be Natasha and then the second person was Aiyanna. Next, I was shocked to hear that I would be running in third, with Kyra running in anchor—the final leg. I hadn't run third ever at that point. I usually would run the first leg for Team Canada or anchor when I was back in Maryland, because anchor is usually reserved for the strongest runner. Third is so different: you're taking the baton and you're passing it. I could do both, but I'd never done both in one race, and we hadn't practiced that part at all at that point.

Aiyanna, who I was going to be taking the baton from, and I got to practice the handoff once. I remember one of the alternate girls who wasn't going to be running actually questioned my hand-off as we practiced. She told me I was doing it wrong and I should do it a different way. I was so confused. But instead of arguing with her or starting to get freaked out, I just took a breath and walked over to the coach. I asked him if he saw our handoff, and he said yes. I asked if there was anything wrong with it. He said no. And that was the end of the conversation.

In that moment, I felt so proud that I finally could stand on my own. I was like, 'No, I got this spot. You're not gonna tell me just out of the blue that I'm not doing something right when I actually *was* getting it right.' That girl didn't realize it, but she did me a huge favor: it made me think, 'I deserve this spot.'

From the time the order is decided until the start of the race itself is shorter than you'd expect, but on this day, it felt much longer. We're waiting in the holding area with all the other nations —there are a huge number of countries represented—and our start was delayed because the javelin thrower from India was throwing really well and it was taking a little longer.

I remember just getting up and doing high knees, feeling really strong and ready. I looked over at my teammates and we all seemed to be feeling the same way. We gave each other these little nods that clearly said 'We're good.'

Walking on to the track felt different. We walked out onto that field at night, but we couldn't tell that the sky was dark because the lights on the Birmingham track were so bright. These huge white lights kind of blur the audience into one huge crowd. When I say the crowd was massive, I mean it was truly huge. Before the races, they actually added more stands there to increase the capacity to over 30,000 people. When I tell you that as soon as the gun went off, you literally felt the vibration from the cheering, all in one single roar... it was incredible. There is so much adrenaline pumping.

It's free energy when you're surrounded by people screaming and cheering for you. The crowd forces you wide awake. It was the most alert I've ever been, which is really good for a night race because it's easy to start getting drowsy while you're waiting. But it was so loud, so bright, so alive.

We walked out onto the track and it's *really* cold in England, even in August, when the sun goes down. We were put in order by the track, and my teammate was shaking. I put my hand on her back. And in that moment, I felt like I was truly part of this team, in this magical moment.

I found myself suddenly having this wave of positive self-talk sweeping through my mind—'you're going to do this, you're going to do great'—and I remember thinking, 'it's been too long since I thought this way.'

Even in a crowd of 30,000, before our start, there was this hush, like everyone was holding their breath. Our first runner Natasha is in our blocks and when the gun went off, it felt like an exhale and everything sprang into motion. Natasha came through in third as she finished her 400. Aiyanna took the baton and went. We stayed in third. When my hand was about to close over the baton, I remember thinking, 'make sure you don't lose contact.' I got the baton and went. Running, running, running, staying tight on Jamaica's runner until the very end, when we passed the batons to our teammates at the same time.

It's amazing how you're going as fast as you can, but you also feel like you're in slow-motion, and you're so aware of everything happening. When I was coming around the curve towards the finish, I realized that I had the baton exactly halfway in my hand—which is not what you want. You want to give your teammate as much room as possible to grab it. So I'm running and trying to slip the baton slowly down in my hand, praying that I wouldn't drop it. I was chanting, 'Don't let up, don't let up,' as I tried to stay in contact with the Jamaican runner while also focusing on getting ready for the handoff, while also trying to figure out how to make sure to give the other runner room for her handoff so we had space for ours. I was so focused on all of these things, in this state of just pure energy, and we connected. When I let it go, it was the greatest sense of relief I've ever felt.

Later, my teammate who received the baton, Kira, said she realized the second before I gave her the baton that we were there. We were in *contention*. I did my job.

Coming from Worlds in Oregon, where I felt like I didn't fulfill my purpose, to feeling as though I did exactly what I was meant to do, giving that baton to Kira, our strongest runner, and giving her that confidence to know she was in a good spot—it felt incredible.

Now, it may not sound like much, her saying that we were in contention for the win after my part of the run. But coming from her, someone that accomplished, someone who I know wouldn't say something just to say it, it meant everything.

It was such such a dramatic finish, because it was a photo finish. But not only was it a photo finish, when they first announced the results, they had us in second. When the judges looked at the replay a bit later, the second runner for England actually stepped out of the line. So the English team was eliminated, and we were bumped up to gold.

We *won*.

But by the time the judges made that call, we were downstairs in the locker room already, and when the official came in to tell us, we exploded. We were screaming and crying and laughing, but I don't think we really believed it until we got up on the podium, and I heard the Canadian national anthem playing. It was the first time I'd heard it on a podium, because I hadn't had a title before that.

You really do have to love your sport to stay in it, but here's the thing: getting the gold does matter. Track is so black and white when it comes to your time. I know that I have value outside of the sport as a person, but really, when it comes to track, it does come down to: 'Are you fast enough?' This gold medal symbolizes all the hard work, all the hours I put in. It symbolizes that I didn't give up in 2019, when everything felt like it was spiraling downward and I wasn't really sure of my talent.

So yes, feeling like I was finally part of the team, that I belonged there, was partially because of the gold. There was an external validation. But the sense of belonging came before I knew what our result was: it came the moment we finished the race as a true team who executed their plan in harmony together. It was the fact that we all felt like we had committed to running as fast as we could. We did this collectively. There was elation from getting gold, but also the realization that we're all the same, that we wouldn't let up. *That* was what gave us the opportunity to win, and that was what mattered the most.

It helped me finally *know*, 'You do have a place on the team. You have so much value.' I think a lot about opportunity in this sport. You do have to make tough choices, and sometimes it's not always the best idea to go to a race. I could have gone home after Worlds and that would have been a logical decision. It was unconventional to be asked at the last minute, to show up and not know if I would have a chance to run or not.

But that's the thing about life. It's never gonna be as clear cut as you want it to be. I don't know what would have happened if I said, 'No, I'm not going to go to Birmingham. It's way too short notice, I'm not ready.' But going made me learn that I can be very adaptable. I can have that confidence. And I can—and do—belong here.

SPRINT THROUGH YOUR SETBACKS JOURNAL PROMPTS

Grab a notebook or just jot your ideas down on these pages!

DEFINE BELONGING FOR YOU

- What does belonging mean to you?
- When have you felt like you have/haven't belonged?
- What would belonging look like, if you don't currently feel like you're part of something?
- What are the internal/external markers you associate with belonging?
- What can you control about feeling like you belong?
- What can't you control—and how can you let go of that?

(And remember, it's normal to feel like you don't belong at different points in your life! We can work on it—it's not the end of the world!)

THINK ABOUT YOUR CURRENT CREW

Remember, people don't need to be chasing the same goals as you to align with your values. You might be trying to achieve greatness on the track while your bestie runs for student body president. But you both love focusing on getting the best out of yourselves and the people around you. Yes, on paper your goals are different... but your values are the same.

- What are your top values?
- Who are your five people you spend the most time with?
- Do you feel like the people you hang out with complement those values? Are they people who align with you achieving your goals? (If not, this doesn't mean ditching your current friend group—but it might mean branching out and meeting some new people!)

- Are you bringing your best to your group? If not, how can you start?

CHOOSE YOUR INNER CIRCLE

- Who's your "team"? If you don't have an actual team, who are your friends/family/coach/teachers etc. who make you feel the most capable of achieving your goals?
- When was the last time you communicated your goals to them? If it's been a while, it might be time for a goal refresh session!

PAUSE

WINDSOR OPEN | ONTARIO, CANADA | 2023

"I have learned over the years that when one's mind is made up, this diminishes fear; knowing what must be done does away with fear."
—*Rosa Parks*

Some races are pivotal because they produce the results that change the trajectory of your career. This race was pivotal because it showed me something even more important: choosing to *not* start a race can be just as critically important to your career—and your health, and your life. You have to know when a pause is necessary so that when it is time to push yourself forward, you're ready for it.

Running professionally is like anything else in life in that it's very up and down, and on the track, it's extremely apparent when things are not going according to plan. Even a small injury can mean the difference between making a team or getting sidelined. Unfortunately, small injuries also tend to come in waves. You recover from one, and then another pops up.

I try to be an optimist about most things, including injuries. My mantra has always been that I'm stepping back in order to spring forward—even if it doesn't feel like that in the moment. And in the summer of 2023, I had to figure out where the line was between being smart about dealing with injuries versus pushing forward in hopes of having a good enough result to keep the Olympic dream alive. That meant learning to say no, even when it was really difficult to make that decision in the moment.

I had suffered a hamstring tear in April of 2023 racing the first weekend at Louisiana State University. After the race, my hamstring felt a bit off and before I knew it, I couldn't run without pain. Fast forward to the second weekend at LSU, it was the first time I ever had to sit out of a meet due to injury—the pain was just too great. It was the obvious choice, the only choice. In the moment, it made me feel like I did something wrong. When I came home, I had an X-ray and MRI to confirm that I had torn my hamstring. Not bad enough for surgery, but I needed some time off to let it heal.

After a few weeks, things seemed to feel better and I headed to a more local race, the Windsor Open. Things weren't feeling quite right, something still felt off in my hamstring. But Windsor was on the schedule, and so I headed to the race hoping that it would work out.

This race was just a few weeks ahead of Canadian Nationals, which was my focus for the year. When we laid out my initial schedule, Windsor was set to be my primary tune-up race where we dialed in the last block of racing and training before Nationals. With track and field, generally you want to be racing regularly versus taking prolonged breaks in between races. Marathoners may only do a couple races per year, but track athletes need races in order to stay sharp. This race also would be a good test for Nationals because a lot of the women who were racing at Nationals would be on the start line with me. We don't always have similar schedules, so it's hard to know how well everyone is doing—this was a perfect chance to check out the competition and make some tactical tweaks for Nationals.

This was my second 400-meter race after tearing my hamstring. The week before, I'd had a solid race with one of my best starts I'd ever had. In that race, I actually led through the first 300 meters and only got passed at the very end, where I felt like I'd run out of energy. The girl who won ran a really, really fast time, but I still felt a little discouraged because normally, my last 100 is my strongest and I was concerned about that feeling of low energy. My coach wasn't worried about it—he was proud of me for executing the fast start—but I was nervous for what the last part of the race would mean for me at Nationals. I just couldn't see that race the way my coach did, so I was really counting on racing at Windsor to snap me out of that feeling. I had entered that race feeling like I was at this point where I would shine and break through. It felt like I could have done so much more at that last race and I needed a strong finish.

Ultimately, I was putting a lot more pressure on my comeback than was necessary. So it shouldn't have been a surprise that when I went to Windsor for the race, things were boiling up and about to explode. I had talked myself back into feeling ready to try again and I was in pretty good spirits, despite some lingering doubts. This was a track I'd raced on before, so I was feeling more prepared and confident. The only problem was that my hamstring was still tight after the last race. Still, I ignored it until we were on the track doing a warmup. There, I couldn't hide. It started as just a tingle, but it progressively got tighter and tighter. I was doing all of my usual tactics to stay in a good headspace. I had really fun hiphop playing in my headphones, I was telling myself to 'put your best foot forward, just have a smooth race…'

But in the back of my mind, I could just tell that my hamstring just didn't really want to go. I tried to deny it but I couldn't get it to the full range that I needed it. I went to do a few strides, but couldn't get up to full speed. The doubt was starting to trickle in—not just that it was going to be a bad race, but that the race itself could really hurt me.

As I kept going in my warmup, I was feeling more tightness in my leg to the point where I couldn't get my stride as open as it usually is. When I cut my stride down, I'm actually changing the way that I run significantly, since my long stride is my signature style. And it was getting worse. With every step, I could feel the rest of my body adjusting to work around that hamstring, and I realized that I was trying to protect myself and I was focusing on that instead of just running.

It was decision time. Yes, I could hobble through the race. But the purpose and the goal of that race wasn't to make it to the finish line, the goal was to push and have a good effort heading into Nationals. I knew it wasn't going to be a good effort. There was no way that I was going to produce a 50-point-something second run where I qualified for the Olympics and my whole career would be made from that. Looking at that, it was obvious that racing didn't make sense. But that didn't make it easier to drop out.

My coach noticed that something was clearly wrong and he tried to give me a pep talk, but when I went to do one more stride, I had no speed. I couldn't push. My brain was blocked, my hamstring was tightening up even more, and I felt like I was crashing. I did one more stride. It didn't feel good. And then, I simply sat down and I started crying. It felt like there was way too much emotion for this moment.

The warmup period ended with me sitting there, thinking about what to do, and I only had a few minutes to make the decision: should I pull out of the race? It felt dramatic. I was signed up and checked in, and the race started in less than 20 minutes. If I raced, I'd be finished in less than 21 minutes! All I had to do was walk over to that final check in, and get ready to do my best.

But I couldn't do it. I had this feeling that if I tried to push through and do the race, I would make my hamstring so much worse, potentially making a race at Nationals impossible. I still dreaded walking over to the registration table to let them know I wasn't racing. It was so much harder than just going through the motions of racing. But it was the right thing to do. I walked over and told them I wouldn't be starting. And of course, they asked if I was sure, and I was trying not to start crying again as I said I was positive. It was almost harder because I've raced there before so the volunteers all knew me and they were sad for me.

I walked away by myself, trying to keep my emotions in check. As I was trying to tell myself that yes, I did do the right thing by not racing, I decided I would give my chiropractor—the one I'd been working with on the hamstring tear—a call to see what he thought. We'd worked together since 2017, so he knows me really well. I called him up and explained the situation. He said, "Micha, I think that you just saved yourself for the season, maybe even for your career."

Instantly, I felt validated, and like a weight had been lifted off of my shoulders. My coach had been okay with my decision, but he didn't really understand how I was feeling. My chiropractor did. He told me to come see him the next week and to be careful with my hamstring until then. He also told me to cancel any upcoming races. We scrapped the next couple of weeks—no decisions or maybes about it, just no racing. I felt the pressure lift.

Sometimes, you do need that other person validating your decisions in order to feel okay about them. There's no shame in that, but you do want to make sure you have the right people in your corner if you know that's how you think and feel. My coach was great and he was fine with my decision, but he didn't fully understand it. My teammates might support my decision, but they also have their own agendas in racing—which is totally reasonable. Calling my chiropractor in that moment was exactly the right decision for me. I was looking for validation, yes, but I didn't want to call someone who would just tell me that I did the right thing without really understanding what was going on. I was looking for an educated, supportive response. I know if I had called my mom, she would have been supportive, but she also would have consoled me and agreed with me that I made the right call even if she doubted it. But I wanted someone who would be unbiased and who had more of the facts—my chiropractor had been working with me on my hamstring, so he understood what I was talking about.

Instead of racing for the next three weeks, we were all about rehabbing my hamstring while working on my mental game. The hamstring had really highlighted a lot of my mental weaknesses: when things were going well, it was easy for me to be feeling positive and trust myself, but with the injury, my mindset started shifting to more negative territory. Since I wasn't able to really push myself in workouts or races before Nationals, my mental game needed to be as dialed as possible if I had any chance of racing well there. We could hopefully get my hamstring to a place where I could race well at Nationals without risking further injury, but it would be my mind that would lead to the best result, not my legs.

The goal became about going to Nationals as my best self—the best self that I was in that moment, not my best self ever, not the best self from 2016 or any other year. This was going to be the year where I just ran my best with a hamstring that was in the process of healing. Once I was able to come to that understanding, it was easier for me to step back and not be so critical of myself.

I looked at the calendar with my coach and my chiropractor, and we figured out just how much I needed to race and train in order to be in the best position possible heading into Nationals. It was going to be tight, but we made a calendar that made sense for rehab, training, and the bare minimum of racing needed to tune up. I did start racing a couple of weeks ahead of Nationals just to get back on a start line, and honestly, it didn't feel great. I was over-thinking every race, constantly assessing how I was feeling. But I knew I was healed to the point where I wasn't risking my season by doing those races, and that I needed an actual race time to know that I could at least hit a 53 at Nationals. I needed to test and push it, because you can't go from zero to Nationals.

My chiropractor and I worked hard on rehab in that time as well and by the time I was getting on the flight to Nationals, I was feeling like I had a chance. I knew winning was out of the question, but I thought I could do well enough to stay in the game heading into an Olympic year.

The first hurdle: getting into the finals at Nationals. That had become my primary goal, rather than winning the 400 meter at Nationals. If I at least managed to make it to the finals, that would be good enough to show that I was still an Olympic hopeful. To me, it was the minimum viable goal. At the track, my warmups were feeling good. Not amazing, but no pain. By the time I got into the blocks for that first qualifying race, I knew my goal was just to do what I could and to push as hard as I could to make it to the finals. It would be a gamble. I might hurt my hamstring and not be able to race well in the finals if I pushed too hard, but if I didn't give it my all, I may not even get to the finals so I'd miss the chance to try. I was going to have to race this qualifier as though it was the final event.

The race started and I didn't have a great first 200 meters. I was falling behind. But here's the thing: this time, I was playing it exactly as I planned it. Knowing I have a good finish, believing in that, I decided that my best strategy was to go out a bit conservatively and then push myself as hard as I could in the last 200 meters. It was my best chance of my hamstring holding up, and I knew it was important to believe in my ability to finish strong. The mental work we'd done in the past month was paying off.

Not only did I have enough to finish, I surged through a few of the girls—some who were ranked higher than me—and finished high enough to secure my spot in the finals. In that moment, even with my hamstring pinging with a little pain, I knew that undoubtedly, I'm here to stay. I'm all in on this sport.

That evening, even with finals happening the next morning, I felt this incredible sense of calm. I looked out my hotel room window and saw the big moon and I had this sense that it was a good omen. Things were going to work out. Fast forward to finals the next day: The gun goes, and I charge out as fast as I can, and this time, I'm not really thinking tactics, I'm just thinking, 'Go as hard as you can until you cross the finish line.' It's not my most explosive or aggressive start, but it's strong and more importantly, I feel strong. With 100 meters to go, I'm sitting in seventh. Not bad, but it's also not where I need to be. I could do more.

Afterwards, my coach admitted that at 300 meters into the race, he was very nervous. He claimed I was giving him a heart attack. But what he didn't realize was that I was feeling ready to go. In that last month of working on my mental game, I'd remembered what I love about who I am as a runner: I don't give up. Moments like these are just opportunities to do something big.

I surged through girl after girl in that last 10 seconds, moving from seventh place up to fourth. It wasn't the result I was hoping for at the beginning of the season, but still nursing my hamstring tear, it was solid. I was back.

When you hit that pause point, your brain instantly goes to the worst case scenario. For me, that was, 'What if this means I can't run the rest of my season? What if this means I can't make the Olympic team?' That headspace is the most dangerous place to be —and because as runners, we have injuries pretty frequently, if every little thing puts you into that mindset, you're not going to get very far.

It's hard to accept any time off, especially when it's unplanned, but it's normal. You can use that time to grow, or you can use that time to let that worry and anxiety build. I'd rather grow. I'd rather use the time to get stronger mentally as well as physically, and to really tune into learning more about the sport. That looks like watching old races I've done and assessing those, working on my goal-setting, planning out the season. And the time off also means more time for sleep, meal prep, all that kind of stuff that we sometimes struggle with when it's busy.

Opting out of a meet doesn't have to be a defining moment for you. But it can be a pivotal one if you know that the strongest thing that you can do that day is to *not* race.

There is a delicate balance in life when it comes to pushing through something that's hard versus knowing when it's time to back off. When you have a big project due for school or work but you're not feeling good, you have to assess whether or not you'll be able to push through and finish the project in any kind of quality way, or if you're going to turn in a sloppy mess. If it's going to be a mess, it's time to ask for an extension. You can't do that all the time, obviously. There are times you do have to push beyond where it's comfortable. But pushing doesn't always get you to the finish line.

If it's an all-or-nothing big deal project, it's better to ask for that extension and be able to turn in a great project a few days later. This was me at Windsor: cancel that race in order to have my best shot at a great result at Nationals. But if it's not a big deal if the project is a little sloppy and you really just need a result, it's time to push and get it done. For me, that looks like racing when I have a cold or a headache, but I know I need to do this semi-final race to qualify for the finals. It's not going to be my best effort but I can get it done.

You need to be able to ask yourself (and maybe your boss or teacher!): "Would you rather I hand in a really sloppy rush job now, or do the project to the best level that I can produce by the end of next week?" And you need to be able to assess what will happen if you turn in something rushed or sloppy versus asking for that extension. In the moment, it may seem smart to just rush through something to get it done and check off the box. But sometimes, sloppy work is worse than turning something in late, or not at all.

For me, I knew if I did that race at Windsor, I'd likely run a really slow time for me, maybe a 56-second run. And that 56 would be listed on my ranking. If I didn't race, there wouldn't be a time listed, so in this case, there was actually a worse consequence to racing versus sitting it out. Racing wouldn't have been strategic—a slow time on your rankings can be bad for getting selected to teams because it can make you look less consistent. So I want to make sure every run that I do is the highest quality possible.

In this sport, we are ultimately our own managers and our own head coaches. (And the same is true for our lives—I love the saying that you're the CEO of your company, and your company is you!) So in that moment of deciding not to race, I'm trying to think like a CEO: I'm looking at all of the potential outcomes and what they would do for my future as a runner. If I run, I might have a slow time that brings my ranking down. I might injure my leg much worse. I might have a surprisingly great race, of course, but I knew that was the least likely outcome. Choosing not to run was the best choice for future Micha.

Not every race decision is like that: I absolutely have made the opposite decision and ran even when I wasn't feeling my best. In the early season of 2021, when we were just getting back to racing after COVID, I had been training primarily on the indoor track in Canada and was at my first race back on an outdoor track after nearly a year. I was racing some of the best girls in the US, girls who had been training in Florida and other warm places, so they'd already been doing a lot of work on the outside track where the turns are smoother and the surface is slightly different.

And here I was, placed in my least favorite lane—lane one—and my hip was feeling tight. It was bothering me from doing so much indoor running, with those sharp turns and the need to lean into the corners the same way every time. I definitely was feeling it in my warmup… But I was also looking around, seeing all these girls who put up times that are so much faster than mine.

I shook it off and tried to do an assessment as my own coach/manager/CEO. My hip wasn't truly in that much pain, it was just a little uncomfortable. Really, I was just feeling intimidated. But I knew that getting in a solid race would do a lot more for my confidence than dropping out and I knew I could run a decent time. I told myself to just have fun, to be excited and proud to be able to line up with all of these fast girls.

I did not win. In fact, I came in last. But I did get out there and try—and my time wasn't too bad. It was a perfect example of my brain trying to make excuses so that I could drop out. This was a chance to rise to an opportunity rather than hit pause, though. And it can be hard to tell the difference. That's why you need to get good at being your own manager, to be able to step back from your initial reaction, assess how you're actually feeling, look at how your decision now could impact your future… and then choose the best option that you can in that moment. It won't always be the right choice, but approaching a choice like that from all angles at least gives you the best chance of choosing the right option for you.

SPRINT THROUGH YOUR SETBACKS JOURNAL PROMPTS

Grab a notebook or just jot your ideas down on these pages!

FIND THE POSITIVE IN SAYING NO

Look for times in your life where saying no has worked out for you.
  1.
  2.
  3.
  4.

PRACTICE YOUR "NO"

A lot of us struggle to say no. Consider this your chance to practice!

- Write down a few common things you get asked to do that you'd rather say no to (like another horror movie marathon with a friend when you hate horror movies!).
- How do you normally respond to those situations? Look through emails and texts to see how you've responded in the past. Are you apologetic but kind of say no? Do you say yes in the moment but get grumpy about it later?
- What are three ways you could say no instead? I love an unapologetic 'no' that also offers the option you're willing to do. For example, I was feeling under the weather because I had such a big week. I texted my coach, "Hey, Coach, I'm taking Monday off because I don't feel great. I'm going to use the extra day to relax and recover. I'll see you Tuesday." I wasn't apologizing, I didn't offer a big explanation—I was just clear about saying no to practice on Monday, and gave him my solution, which was to shift practice to Tuesday instead.

REFRAME YOUR NO'S FOR *YOU*

This part isn't how to say no—it's how to see the no's as a positive! Look at the examples you just came up with, those times you struggled to say no. How would saying no actually benefit the person you're turning down?

- For the horror movie-loving friend, maybe your 'no' prompts them to find a local club of horror movie lovers who actually want to sit around and discuss *Friday the 13th*.
- When I told my coach I needed to skip practice on Monday, I'm helping him do his job by ensuring that I don't end up sick.
- If your friends want to go to a fancy restaurant that you can't *really* afford with your current budget, that's a hard one to say no to! But if you say yes and then are stressed out at dinner the entire time (and ordering just an appetizer when they're all doing three-course meals!), they're not going to have much fun either.

FIND YOUR "YES" TRIGGERS

Now, it's time to think about what makes you say 'yes' automatically, so that you can spot it and make a thoughtful decision based on the outcome you actually want.

- What triggers bring on the feelings of having to do something? Has that led to bad outcomes? How does it feel in those moments in your body? Do you get sweaty? Does your heart rate increase?
- Be ready to take a step back: what are basic questions you can ask yourself to bring you back into the moment? Write them down so you remember them. (Questions like 'how do I actually feel?' or 'do I have time in my

schedule for that?' are great options since they force you to step back and objectively survey the scene.)

- What's a simple mantra/reminder to remember for these moments? ('Pause' is a great one!)

DEFINE FUTURE YOU

When I opted to not race at Windsor, I told myself that "Choosing not to run was the best choice for Future Micha." Now, it's your turn: who is Future You? Describe her! Get as detailed as you want, and go as far into the future as you want. Maybe Future You is just a year from now, maybe she's 10 years old. Find what feels right for you!

Once you define your Future You, keep a few notes about her somewhere you see regularly, like your mirror in the bathroom, your locker or your journal. Whenever you're making decisions, try to bring Future You to mind: what would she say or do?

STYLE

"My mission in life is not merely to survive, but to thrive; and to do so with some passion, some compassion, some humor, and some style."
    –Maya Angelou

What does style have to do with running? It may seem unrelated, but I believe that style and the 'you' that you present to the world can change how you step up to the starting line. If you don't think style matters for you, consider this: Think back to a time you felt incredibly uncomfortable or awkward. You probably were wearing something that felt completely out of place and not like you or the clothing itself was really uncomfortable. For me, I think about being back in fifth grade and trying to fit in with the style then, with big basketball shorts and white tank tops. That didn't make me feel powerful. It made me feel like I was pretending to be a different person.

When I was younger, before I ever started thinking about racing, I was obsessed with Serena Williams and Florence Griffith

Joyner (AKA Flo-Jo). To me, they both had this incredible style, but more than that, they had a power and energy about them. Looking back, Black women athletes have always led the style charge—and now we see it in athletes like women's track superstar Sha'Carri Richardson. I can't think of any athlete who pushed style in sport as much as Flo-Jo did with her one-piece suit with the one full leg. Then there was Serena, kicking off controversy with her catsuit at the French Open in 2018 that baffled reporters and almost got her fined. And now, Sha'Carri has really made wearing your natural hair on the start line a statement... but just as important, she's made it normal to wear it dyed a bright red or in a fun style. She's embracing whatever style she's feeling on that day and I love that.

For me, Serena was the first example I saw of a Black woman both playing sports *and* being a style icon. She made me feel like I could wear the beads in my hair and still be taken seriously as an athlete. As a Black girl growing up, I always put beads and clips in my hair, dangling at the end of my braids. I didn't see that a lot around me or in the media, so to see her on this world stage completely owning it, it showed me what was possible. It brought me so much joy and even pride. It was like, "Whoa, she can have her natural hair and be revered and not have to try to be like somebody else." We just didn't have as many role models as we do today that are bringing their own style.

Having women like her in sport is so important because it reminds us that we can wear so many styles, we can have so many personas, and we can bring what we need in order to perform at our best. Women are able to speak with our personal style. We're able to embrace our personal style and showcase it on the start line. I love being able to blend being feminine with being athletic—and I love that you don't need to choose between those two.

I gain so much confidence when I spend time on my style, deciding what to wear that feels good and expresses how I'm feeling that day. And I'll be honest, I know that when I feel good, when I look good, those are the days where I perform the best at practice. I love that US Open-winning tennis player Coco Gauff told a reporter that in the middle of a set when she was nervous, she just thought, "I feel good, I look good," and that relaxed her. She often mentions that she loves makeup and fashion, and I love that that can be part of her brand beyond tennis.

In the past, we have struggled to be taken seriously if we focus on our appearance but that shouldn't take away from the hard work that we do. It seems like our generation of women, especially Black women, are now leaning in and saying, "I can be so many different things. I'm multifaceted." You can be super stylish, or not. You can do your nails, or not. You can do your makeup, or not.

When I first started, I had to identify and find who I wanted to portray on race day. At first, I was always so nervous, I didn't want anything out of the ordinary. But now, I love getting my hair done in cornrows or nice braids, having my makeup done, having my nails done, because I feel more confident. I can tell myself, "You're going to run well, and you're going to look great doing your post-race interview." In a way, having that style is manifesting my result. It's taking an action based on the belief that I'm going to do well and that I'm going to have all eyes on me.

There's your everyday style, what you wear for a normal lower-key race, and then there's the serious finals outfit, the one you put on when you know you need to really *show up*. For me, that's my orange one-piece from New Balance right now. If anybody sees me at a race and they see me in that one-piece, they know I'm going to be bringing it. It creates this positive pressure for me. It's the choice that I'm making. And if I want to show up and perform, why not stand out while I'm doing it?

Personally, I want to embrace the narrative that athletes who aren't afraid to feel good, look good and stand out will run faster. And maybe they're going to rub some people the wrong way, but that's okay. People talk about Sha'Carri, but I'd rather have people talking about me rather than not knowing who I am. If people aren't talking about you, what are you doing? We're in a sport that is full of people who are so, so fast. You need to be able to stand out.

Personally, I feel much more put together when I have my nails done. I've always worn them long, and people have always commented on them.

Style helps you visualize an outcome in more detail too: at Canadian Track and Field Nationals in 2023 in Langley, British Columbia, I got my nails done in a sparkly orange, and that was intentional. I saw Future Micha wearing her orange nails with her one-piece track suit and looking so fire, so strong, so confident. 'We're going to *work* at Nationals,' I thought, and I wanted to put myself in the best power position and confident headspace possible.

I love stepping onto the track, taking off my warmup suit that's over my race kit, and feeling like I'm stepping into that persona.

It really is something big when you know you want to be your best self and you want to take up space and be seen for who you are. You're doing it for yourself. There's a shift that happens when you decide that you're ready to take up space, and that you're ready for people to see you for who you are. When I'm wearing something eye-catching at practice or in a race, I'm saying, "Don't look away. This is going to be something special. This is going to be a big effort."

You want to have eyes on you, you want people to look, and when you have those eyes on you, you know you have to put together something special in your race. And I think one influences the other: you have more eyes on you, so you push yourself a little bit harder, and as you run faster, more people will notice you.

This is a champion mentality. Champions don't think 'I don't want anyone to notice me.' Champions think, 'Yeah, you're going to want to take that picture.'

When I was on that start line in my orange one-piece, I showed up as my full self. I was confident, I was comfortable, and I was ready to perform. Even though I was injured, I had the best race of my career in the 200-meter, because I felt the most like myself.

I ran that 200-meter semifinal in 23.30. That run got me into the finals, and I finished fourth there as well—which served as a good reminder to me that the 400 isn't the only option for me. It was my best finish in an individual Canadian Championship race.

My 200 probably went better than it would have before my hamstring injury just because I was able to relax and enjoy it. I felt like I had more speed because most of the training I did heading into Nationals was shorter and punchier in order to not push a lot of volume on my hamstring. That race felt like a gift, and it all came down to having that confidence.

Style goes far beyond what you're wearing. You can be wearing the exact same outfit as the girl next to you, but give it a completely different style. Style is about more than your clothes, it's about your essence. Style really encompasses your whole aura, the way people view you when you walk into a room, and the feeling that sticks with people when you leave. I think that people should lean into that, especially in the world of high performance, whether that's in the business world, or school, or on the track.

I think about getting to watch Serena Williams play in person years ago: I remember thinking she was just so focused and in her element, even during her warmup. Her style was more than what she was wearing, it was how she was standing, how she was speaking, how she was making people around her feel. She exuded this confidence and power, and I believe that's intentional on her part and it's part of why she dresses the way she does.

When I think about my style, I think about how I want to look and be perceived, but I also think about how I want to feel, both emotionally and physically. Before I run, I want to feel comfortable, I want to feel confident, and I want to feel relaxed. I want to show up to the start line feeling pumped up, but in a controlled way. Even the music you have playing in your headphones that no one else can hear contributes to your style. Sure, people can't see it, but they can see you reacting to it, even if it just shifts your demeanor from calm to focused or excited.

Your style is also your energy. You know how when someone is super negative all the time, it doesn't matter what they're wearing, they always just give off that negative vibe? The opposite can be true too. I'm a really positive person, so part of my style is about bringing good energy to every situation.

This goes beyond sport, too: if you're reading this and you're a high school student or working from home, you can shift your style to show up as the student or employee that you want to be. Maybe you have a pair of clear glasses or a certain sweater that you wear for test day at school or for big work sessions where you need to be fully focused. That's your orange one-piece. You're creating a persona, the fully realized, fully confident version of yourself who shows up to get work done.

To find your own style, think about what pieces of clothing you own already that really speak to you. When was the last time you felt extremely powerful and confident? What were you wearing? Was it the color that popped? Or was it the type of clothing? You may realize you have a few styles that go with your different personas: maybe you have that power outfit that helps you take a math test, but you also have that shorts and singlet set that you wear when you want to absolutely slay that workout. There will probably be similarities, like a color or the way clothing fits. For me, when I'm thinking about my style, I think about having one color that pops. It may be a fully monochromatic outfit in one great color, or it might be wearing a lot of neutrals and then one piece with a really loud color that pops. I definitely know that being colorful is my true essence.

When I was first racing, I thought I had to wear black all the time. Everyone else did, so it became my uniform. But looking back, when I was a kid, I remember that I loved purple. So one day, I decided to wear a full purple outfit to practice. Everyone freaked out! They loved it. And I realized that I was telling myself this false narrative that wearing purple would be weird and people wouldn't get it and I'd feel uncomfortable, but no—it made me feel so much more powerful and like the best version of myself.

When I was younger, I loved any color. Everything was bright. I had a Bedazzler and everything had jewels all over it. And yes, obviously you can't race with rhinestones everywhere. But what if, at a track meet, you have some rhinestones on your face or on a headband? You're refining the things that made you so happy and feel so good about yourself when you were young, and bringing them into who you are now. You're creating your signature.

When you're able to play with your style and find what feels the most powerful, the most like you, that's when you become the most confident version of yourself. Maybe it's a t-shirt and jeans, or maybe it's a full face of makeup. No one else can define your style for you. You have to embrace all parts of yourself, and let them shine through.

Your style—at its loudest—should be something that makes you feel like you can go into a room and cause a little bit of discussion, but it still allows you to focus on the task at hand. My orange one-piece is exactly that: it's my loud pop of color, turned up to 11. On a daily basis, I'm not wearing that, but I will add in something bright to whatever I'm wearing.

Finding your power uniform may take some work if you don't have one in mind. It might be a color you love to wear—I love coor-dinating my whole outfit into a monochrome statement. Maybe it's your nails, or your hair, or a piece of jewelry. It doesn't have to be extreme. It should make you feel the most comfortable, the most yourself in your body. But make sure it makes you stand out a little bit. We get so swept up in trends and wearing what everyone else is wearing that sometimes, we lose our sense of what truly does make us feel like we're standing in our own power. Stand out the way you want to stand out.

As women, we need to take up more space. It's so easy to feel like blending in is easier. But in sports, why not stand out? When you're standing out, it's easier to be confident and feel like it's your time to shine.

We have this one life: why would we just sit on the sidelines and try to blend in? Remember: look good, feel good, do good.

SPRINT THROUGH YOUR SETBACKS JOURNAL PROMPTS

Grab a notebook or just jot your ideas down on these pages!

DEFINE YOUR IDEAL STYLE

- What do you want your style to say about you? What do you want to tell the world when they see you?
- What pieces/styling elements make you feel most you?
- What words, what moods, what music, what colors signify the 'you' that you want the world to know?
- What is your OUTFIT? You know—the one that makes you feel like you can do anything! (For me, this is my orange one-piece for racing.) You might have a couple for different aspects of your life, like one that makes you feel like a boss for a school presentation versus your race day outfit. But you may notice some similarities between the two in terms of colors and style!

GET UNAPOLOGETIC

As women athletes, we also tend to feel like we "shouldn't" care about our style or wear makeup or do our hair to train or compete. But I feel so much more powerful when my nails are done and my hair is looking great and I have on a bit of (waterproof) makeup. If doing any of that makes you feel more powerful, don't let anyone tell you that you can't!

I know that for me, I gave up wearing really bright colors for a while because all the "serious athletes" wore mostly black. But that's not me! And similarly, I kept my hair really simple for a long time. But my braids are my favorite look—so now, I am unapologetic about them.

We have to talk about being unapologetic with your style. What are things you've been told you "shouldn't" wear? Why?

TAKE YOUR STYLE AND OWN IT

- How can you translate your style to casual, everyday life? Let's be honest, none of us are dressing up every single day—we don't have time for that! But we can make sure everyday, we're adding a little bit of style to our usual uniform. What are little things you can add to everyday looks, like little pops of color or sneaky accessories that don't feel over-the-top (unless that's your vibe, in which case, love that for you!)
- How can you pump it up for "race day"? Take those style prompts and dial them up! (Again, you may have a few different outfits here for different big moments in your life.)

JOY

PALIO CITTA' DELLA QUERCIA | ITALY | 2023

"Don't settle for average. Bring your best to the moment. Then, whether it fails or succeeds, at least you know you gave all you had. We need to live the best that's in us."
— *Angela Bassett*

You wouldn't expect a chapter titled "Joy" to start with a terrible bout of food poisoning alone in a small hotel room in Italy, but here we are.

After Worlds in 2023, where I was once again on the team and at the race but then didn't get to actually run, I knew that I had to keep racing. If I wanted that Olympic spot for Paris 2024, I had to prove that my 52.75 fourth place finish at Nationals earlier in the season wasn't the best time I could run post-hamstring tear.

But back to the food poisoning. The timing couldn't have been worse: I flew to Italy for the Palio Citta' della Quercia race from World Championships in Budapest. I had a few days on my own before my mom arrived, and I planned to spend them being a tourist, doing some active recovery. So I started by taking myself out to dinner: I went to the hotel restaurant, where the pasta was fantastic. The waitstaff was lovely. It was a simple meal, but it was delicious.

My hotel was right in the middle of the city square, and when I first arrived, I spent a couple hours just window-shopping. There were all of these beautiful boutique shops, lots of Louis Vuitton, Prada, Gucci. It was the perfect place to be alone: A small enough city that it wasn't overwhelming, but big enough to feel like I was exploring a new place. And I know just enough Italian to get around, which made it more enjoyable. When you race internationally and that's your primary focus, I think it's important to spend time using apps like DuoLingo to be well-versed in as many languages as possible, since it makes international travel and meets so much more enjoyable. It's freeing when you know a bit of the language.

The second day in Italy, I just had a little shakeout run on the schedule and met up with some other track girls who were in town for the meet the coming weekend. We ended up out to dinner and I got the exact same meal—pasta and some steak. Except this time, the hostess asked if I wanted parmesan. And I remember thinking, sure, that's fine. I'll have parmesan on my pasta.

Now, I can't swear that it was the parmesan, but when I went to bed, I was feeling a bit off. Something just wasn't sitting well in my stomach. I assumed it was from having a couple of travel days and being in a new environment, getting used to everything here.

But no. When I woke up the next morning, I couldn't stop throwing up. There's no way to sugarcoat it, I've never been this sick in my life. I spent the morning on the floor in my bathroom. By the afternoon, it seemed like maybe things were settling down, so I decided to risk going to practice—for some reason, it seemed so important in my head. Big mistake. The entire time driving over to the track, I was just trying not to get sick.

After the 15-minute car ride, I get there and I put my things down, and I try to look calm but quickly aim for the bathroom. I'm sick again. And now I'm worried. This is definitely food poisoning and it is not good.

Still, I'm an elite athlete, and in these situations, we tend to push just a little too hard sometimes and convince ourselves that if we just focus, we can get through stuff like this. So, I clean up and head out to the field. I'm about to start my warmup, but when I try to do my jumps and other dynamic movements to get ready, I can't do it. Even a tiny bounce makes me feel nauseous. I'm doing this tiny little skip and feeling worse and worse by the minute. I don't even know where my body starts or where it ends. And at this point, it's becoming clear that this practice isn't going to work. But I also can't leave and get back to the hotel on my own, so I keep trying to fake it.

I'm just doing the bare minimum, keep going to the bathroom, and then trying to run. It's not working. Finally, I give in and sit down with my stuff, defeated and just ready to get home. But I have an hour and a half left until I'm rescued by our driver, so I end up putting my backpack right next to my head, and I literally just slept for an hour until the car finally came and my stomach did flips the entire drive home.

Back at the hotel, I'd never been so glad to go back to my room. But at this point, I'm also starving. I didn't have breakfast because I couldn't keep anything down. I tried sipping Gatorade at practice, but even that was coming back up. But I didn't have the energy to try to find anything to eat or drink, I just wanted to lie down (after throwing up one more time). I slept for another eight hours, only getting up to rush to the bathroom to throw up, even though I had nothing left in my system.

That hotel room is ingrained in my memory now. It had this great long window so I could see out—even though I had my head buried most of the time I was in there—and a queen sized bed made from two single beds pushed together. There was a tiny hallway between the room and the bathroom, and the bathroom was all this tiled orange granite—so much color for a bathroom!

By eight that night, I woke up again and I realized that I needed to eat or drink something, because the empty stomach was only making the situation worse. So I made my way downstairs and used my high school-level Italian to try to ask for just some toast, explaining that I was sick and that I thought it was something I had eaten. Before I knew it, they put together this tray for me that had this mountain of little bread rolls and tea, and sent it up to my room for me. It was the nicest thing, even though I could only eat a couple bites and drink a bit of the tea.

It was a solitary moment: I don't think you ever feel quite as alone as when you're in a foreign country, don't really speak the language fluently enough to make friends, don't know anyone, and don't feel well. The next day when I woke up, I was feeling better but I still stayed in my room. I had learned my lesson: I could walk around the room without needing to rush to the bathroom, but I wasn't ready to risk practice again. I ate a bit more of the bread and actually went downstairs for some soup. Things were turning around, thankfully.

I went to bed that night feeling pretty normal but completely drained, and when I woke up the next morning, I realized that it was the day before my race already. The last two and a half days had gone by in a total blur. So much for getting in some sightseeing and making my way around town, stopping in sidewalk cafes for the occasional espresso!

I had to get to the track again to get in a bit of pre-race prep, though I felt like I didn't even have enough energy to put on my spikes. My stomach wasn't quite settled after the drive to the track. I kept burping, but at least I wasn't feeling too nauseous, just like something still wasn't quite settled. I definitely wasn't back to my normal health. I just did the best I could, but I couldn't bring myself to push hard enough to even get sweaty. Even bending over to get into my position in the blocks was setting my stomach off and making me nauseous, since you're sort of leaned over and upside down. I'd get down into that position and just stay there, trying to convince myself to get up, but afraid that if I did, I'd be sick. But because it was obvious that I was dealing with food poisoning and not an actual illness, I kept hoping it would pass, and I told myself to feel confident that I'd feel fine on race day. I just tried to keep a brave face and get through practice.

Finally, we were done and I was able to go back to the hotel and settle in with some more soup, trying to keep calm and take in some food. I also had my secret weapon: my mom was arriving that evening, and I knew just seeing her would make me feel better.

I hadn't really talked to my mom much before she arrived. I had texted her about the food poisoning but I didn't give her a lot of details. When she did arrive at the hotel, fresh off the plane, the amount of relief I felt almost instantly was overwhelming. I don't care how old you are, when you're sick and alone, all you really want is your mom to be there for you. And my mom brings such a feeling of calm to any space she walks into. She has such a soothing personality. Her being there made me feel so much better and much more capable of handling this meet. She shifted my whole mood from wallowing in this hotel room with my stuff just sprawled out everywhere, feeling like I had no energy. In the first few minutes, just by moving into the space, she made me feel more energized and grounded.

People have always been surprised at how my mom is so willing to travel to my meets—in college, people would be so shocked that she was there from Canada, especially since their parents were often only a state away and they weren't coming. But mom and I have a different relationship. She's been through what I'm going through. She understands how important it is to have someone there for you—if you look at most of the pro runners out there, they have an entourage with them. They have their coaches, their trainers, their family members or partners or close friends. They know to surround themselves with their most trusted people in order to get their best results. Having that makes a huge difference.

On two bowls of soup over the last three days, I was going to go and race in one of the best, biggest competitions in Italy. But in that moment, I was just thinking that the worst case scenario wasn't so bad. If I couldn't get through the warmup, I promised myself that I would pull out of the race. But if I could warm up without feeling sick, I was going to be fine. And either way, I had my mom there in my corner.

My warmup wasn't as dynamic as I'd like it to be, but I also wasn't nauseous running. It was that fine line between wanting to pull out of the race versus pushing through, and this was one of the times where I knew that pushing through was the right decision for me in that moment. I wasn't going to get sick on the track, I just might be running a little flat. So I told myself that if I can push through a really not-great day like this one, then I would know that I could pretty much race in *any* conditions.

On the start line, I looked around and realized I was starting in lane one—the innermost lane—and I'd be racing some of the fastest 400-meter runners in the world. Running in lane one means you have the tightest, sharpest turns to contend with. And when you have really long levers like I do, it takes longer to turn your legs and get them going in the right direction and it throws off your stride. So when I have a tight turn, it's going to have me lean at a certain angle, just so I can get out of it and onto the straight. The benefit is that you're finished on a straightaway compared to lane eight, which finishes on a slight left turn.

But personally, I prefer lane eight for another reason entirely: I love running scared, with everyone chasing me because lane eight starts so far ahead. In lane one, you don't have anyone starting behind you. You're forced to catch people who are starting further along the track. There's not really a chance for you to be in the mix. You have to try not to focus on everyone in front of you, because you're going to fall into that trap of thinking, 'Is she running fast? Am I running fast? Am I closing on her?' and now you're focused on the wrong thing. The only positive thing is that you do have a better perspective of how the last 100 meters is playing out since you're finishing on a straight, so that helps, but it's still my least favorite lane.

They called "on your marks," and I said to myself, "Okay, let's just see what happens." I stepped into the blocks and this sense of strange calmness came over me. At that point, I just had nothing to lose. When the gun went off, I actually remember having the thought of, 'Oh good, you're running' because I made it out of the blocks and was charging down the track. I had a surprisingly good first 100 meters, but then I felt myself start to fade. My energy stores were just gone. My stomach was bubbling. I was aware of everything that was happening. I was aware of the wind, of my mom, of how the track felt—way more aware than you ever should be in a race like this.

I tried to push harder. I was last heading into the final turn. But I powered through the last straight to finish in 54.1, which wasn't fast by my standards, but at least it wasn't a terrible result that would wreck my rankings. I didn't completely fail.

My mom was so helpful then. She reminded me that I did run well, considering how I was feeling. I wasn't thinking that in the moment, though. I had wanted to have a new personal best in Italy to show the national team what I could do. Instead, I just wanted to go back to the hotel and lie down and have a pity party for myself. But there were so many local children at that meet. It's a small town, and the meet is a really big deal there, so these kids had lined up and they wanted people's autographs—they don't see international athletes every day. I was about to just plow through the crowd and go home, but my mom told me to stop and really *feel* this experience.

As I signed a few autographs for these little kids, I got struck by this intense feeling of gratitude that completely replaced any self-pity that I was feeling. I realized just how lucky I am that I get to travel the world and compete at this high level. This was not my best day. But I showed up, despite everything.

That evening, instead of feeling sorry for myself and staying huddled in my hotel room, I felt a new sense of peace. I had gotten out there and run, and actually had a decent result. I felt brave. And the trip wasn't over. There was still one more shot at redemption. The next morning, we took a bus to an even smaller town in Italy, to another meet. This one was even bigger than the one I had just done, so it was going to be much harder, but there were more points available.

That moment of peace I felt after the first meet didn't last. While the autograph signing had been really fun, I couldn't shake the feeling that I was just not feeling it. When I got to my hotel room in the next town with my mom, I had a bad moment. Honestly, the whole situation had just made everything bubble up inside of me: I was so frustrated with how the season had been going, with the hamstring tear and the comeback and now getting sick, and just not feeling like I was able to really run in the way that I knew I had prepared for. So I was definitely venting a little. (Proving you can be grateful for your life, and still be frustrated!)

I told her I wanted to just stop. I wasn't having fun. I felt like I was just constantly beating myself up. I wasn't enjoying racing. My mom just sat there listening to me, and then she asked me—with no judgment—if I wanted her to tell my agent that I wasn't going to race the next day in the meet.

As soon as my mom asked the question, "Do you want to race?" I contemplated saying no, but I could instantly feel that skipping the meet just didn't sit right with me. I think that her giving me the permission to not run and being so relaxed about it made me really pause and reflect in a rational way. Maybe I just needed to get all of that off of my chest, but after I vented and she asked me that, I felt calm again. And when I thought about it, I realized that I didn't feel comfortable ending my season with a 54-second post-food poisoning run. That wasn't how I wanted to cap the season off. So I told her I was going to race.

The best thing about being an athlete is that you develop the ability to have such foresight into future you. So even though I was having a rough moment, I could still look ahead and see this future version of me walking around in Venice if I decided not to race. How would I feel? I knew that I just wouldn't have felt as fulfilled, I would have felt wrong. There's no way I'd be able to enjoy the experience after calling the end of my season with a very subpar run. I didn't feel comfortable going on a fun trip without giving it my best shot to end the season on a high note. I needed to have a celebration of me running. It might not mean getting a new best time, but I would get out there and do what I could.

My warmup the day before the meet wasn't amazing. I was feeling tight and still nervous about how my stomach was feeling. I was eating again, but it's so hard to replenish three days of not eating anything. But this is where my mom really stepped up. She's my best friend, but she's also my manager and coach in a lot of ways. So she sees me doing my warm up and she starts telling me to open up. Which I get grumpy about, because in that moment, I'm seeing her as an annoying mom telling me what to do when I already know what I'm doing. But then I reminded myself that she's a great person to have with me at these high-intensity meets because she's been there. She's a three-time Olympian. So maybe I *should* listen to her. It's hard when you want to be annoyed that your mom is giving you advice, but the advice she's giving you is super solid and coming from someone who's been in your shoes. She's obviously saying some good stuff.

My relationship with my mom is even more complicated because she's my best friend, but she's also my mentor and someone I look up to. In some ways, it's like having two people in my life: on one hand, she's this young track runner with this huge legacy behind her. And then on the other hand, she is just my mom and my best friend.

Partway through practice, she said, "Tomorrow, all you have to do is make sure that you're opening up, because you're really, really tight." She was right. All that dehydration, all the travel, and all of the stress in addition to still recovering from the hamstring tear were making everything tighter. She can see things that I sometimes miss because she's been there, and because we are so similar. So yes, she was right about my hips. At first I was pushing back against her a lot because no coach has ever mentioned that before. I wasn't in a great place mentally to begin with, so I just wanted her to leave me alone. But she kept pushing it, and finally just asked me to try one time. So fine, I tried doing a few extra deep lunges before my next stride. And she was right, that extra time opening them up made me instantly feel more fluid. So I did listen to her, and it worked.

After that moment, though, she went from being in coaching mode to being in mom mode—because I told her that's what I needed. She may have had more advice, but what I needed from her more was just that support. It's a balance we'll always have to work on, because I know that her knowledge of racing runs so deep and she has such great advice, but at the same time, sometimes I'm not in the place where I can listen to it.

The meet was Wednesday night, and waking up that morning, I finally felt fully back to myself. I felt awake, alert, and *hungry*. My body was finally getting back to the point where I could eat what I wanted. And if I could have more control over my body, I knew I'd gain back some control over my mind. Breakfast and lunch went fine, no issues, and that made me feel so good. I could race on a full stomach.

The location of the meet itself was beautiful: it was set in between a mountain range, right on the Swiss border. I kept thinking, 'You have this chance to race in one of the most beautiful places in the world and you're going to run really well.' That mindset was such a nice shift from where I'd been just days before. Somehow, my mom giving me that permission and approval to choose not running had reminded me how much I do love to race.

At the race venue, there was a lot of confusion when I arrived. They had changed our start time at the last minute, moving it up by 15 minutes. This may not seem like much, but sprinters have super dialed warm-up routines that are timed specifically. 15 minutes is a big deal. So, as soon as I heard that, I needed to start getting ready if I was going to make it to the start. Not a big problem, but it had me a little flustered… though maybe that was a good thing since it gave me less time to be in my head.

As our start time approached, I headed over to the line but there were only a couple of girls there. I guess the message about the earlier time hadn't been very well broadcast—and it didn't make sense anyway, since there was still a race happening on the track. But the other girls all started to come over and they marshaled us all out onto the track, despite the fact that the other race was going on. We were all nervously laughing and just waiting to figure out when we were starting, all while trying to stay loose and ready to race. I was thinking, 'Wow, what a lot of rushing for nothing.' Instead of tensing up though, I remembered my mom's words: open up. In that moment, I didn't think about how that applied to just my hips and my legs, I thought about how it applied to my heart. I started looking around and catching the eyes of my competitors and just laughing a little bit, rolling my eyes, and making jokes about how the race was going to happen at the original time. Everyone seemed to loosen up a little and the atmosphere shifted from being one full of tension to a more relaxed, open vibe.

Finally, we ended up getting called onto the track at the same time we were supposed to there in the first place. I get in my blocks, and I'm realizing that I feel *really* good. Then it was just "Ready-Set-Go!" and we were off and running, and this time, I'm not thinking about everything, I'm only aware of the track in front of me. It was the complete opposite of the meet a couple days earlier. It felt like my mind was like, 'This is your last race of the season, you may as well go for it.' I had a burst of energy in the last 100 meters, and I went from seventh to fourth, hitting my season's best time of 52.38.

When I'm relaxed, when I'm in the moment, when I'm just enjoying the run and the fact that this is what I'm doing in my life, that's when the magic happens. This felt like I had manifested something good out of *enjoying the process.*

The reward for racing was that when we did get to Venice, I was able to fully immerse myself in the experience and just spend that time with my mom enjoying every moment. The roads there are narrow and cobbled and you're walking through these tiny alleyways and over canals on these tiny bridges and it's almost impossible to not get lost. The Venice Film Festival was happening when we were there, so the streets were just swarming with people. Even getting to our hotel was a monumental feat once we got to Venice from the meet: there was a train, two buses and a boat involved. Wild! (And Venice is not a place you want to be dragging two giant roller suitcases, let me tell you.)

In Venice, you go everywhere by boat since there are no cars. It's amazing—and of course, the first thing we did was book a gondola ride. Honestly, it was like a Disney movie. It was so sweet. We actually watched a couple get engaged on another boat that we passed! It felt so picture perfect and after the season I'd had, it felt like I was finally able to completely relax. Over the next couple of days, we wandered the streets, drinking espressos at cafes, eating pasta at restaurants, sauntering through museums looking at all of the amazing art, just soaking in this rich culture and enjoying every second of the off season.

Within five days, that trip went from being the worst way to end the season to finishing with my fastest 400-meter time of the year, all because I was able to release the stress and lean into the joy. From Worlds to food poisoning, it was a chain of events that made me realize that sometimes things can feel a little hopeless. But if you can just shift your mindset and refuse to accept that feeling of hopelessness and embrace joy instead, you can change the outcome. When I can do that, it feels like things are happening *for* me, rather than *to* me. But when I forget that and let myself move into those frustrated emotions, that's when running well feels much harder. Anticipating that something is going to go poorly is so much worse for your mindset than looking ahead and anticipating that things will work out for the best. After that bad moment in the hotel room with my mom, I decided that I'm done feeling bad, I'm done feeling nervous, I'm done feeling scared, I'm done thinking of myself as a small person. I love thinking bigger. I'm meant to be in that space. I always want to be able to look around at my competitors and smile and laugh and joke with them. You can be joyful while still being competitive. The two aren't mutually exclusive. I want to be on every start line with a more open mindset, where I'm asking myself, "Why not run fast?"

SPRINT THROUGH YOUR SETBACKS JOURNAL PROMPTS

Grab a notebook or just jot your ideas down on these pages!

GET READY FOR TOUGH TIMES

- What are a couple of easy ways to make yourself feel instantly a little happier? (I keep a few videos that make me happy on my phone.)
- Who in your life can help shift your mood? (For me, this is definitely my mom!)
- How can you find ways to bring your light into situations? (I remind myself to smile at the people around me, to try to make conversation and just lighten the mood a bit. I always want to contribute positive energy to any situation!)
- Create a routine for when you aren't feeling good: how long do you let yourself have a pity party? How do you snap out of it?

START A GRATITUDE JOURNAL

You've probably heard of gratitude journals already, but they really do work! I try to use mine every day, and just write down a couple of things that I'm grateful for every single morning. Tiny things, big things—whatever feels right for you. It really helps keep things in perspective. Aim for at least three things you're grateful for. You can also think of them as highlights of the day if you don't like starting with "I'm thankful for...". Instead, just write out what your little and big wins from yesterday were! Still stuck? Add one thing you're looking forward to.

WRITE OUT YOUR WHY

It's a lot easier to get through tough moments if you know *why* you're doing something. Having that written down is really help-ful... and you can also use that Why Statement to make yourself some positive affirmations to say every day too! If your *why* is that you want to be the best 400-meter runner that you can be, you can make an affirmation that says "I am a strong, fast runner." Stick that on your mirror so you see it first thing in the morning to keep your goals top of mind!

REFRAME TOUGH MOMENTS

I feel like sometimes, these bad things—like my food poisoning—happen to you because something way better is around the corner. That's my way of accepting whatever is happening to me that might not be ideal. It feels like a more positive way to look at things, and usually it helps me move through those situations faster and with more grace. It's not always possible and it's not always easy, but when you can make it work for you, it can be a seriously helpful skill. In tough times, ask:

- How do I make this moment work for me?
- How can I make this situation better?
- What can I look forward to? (Even something really little!)

EPILOGUE

THE 400-METER IS tough because every race is so different. Not a single race in this book played out the same way as the next. One race isn't going to look the same as another: you might start off really strong in one race, you might start off more conservatively in the next, you might go after somebody in front of you, or you might wait and see until the last 50 meters. You have to look at each race as something unique—you can learn from each time you race, but you can never kid yourself into thinking that you know it all or that there's one formula for success.

I've always had the best results when I've trusted myself and my feelings. Whether that has looked like hard conversations with my coach, telling him that I couldn't run because I knew that I was still in too much pain from my hamstring or tibia injuries, or deciding to push for that faster time when a coach didn't think I could do it, I've always done best when I haven't let other people tell me what I should feel or do.

Letting people dictate your value is such a natural, common thing that we do. In school, so much of our self-worth is wrapped up in grades. At work, it's in promotion or raises. On the track, it's about results and about who gets government funding or sponsor-ship dollars. But that can't be what dictates your self-worth.

You're not only an athlete in this sport. Most of the time, you're your own manager, you're your own agent, you're your own coach, you're your own PR team. You have outside help—I've always had a coach, for example—but they're not full-time staff like you'd have if you played hockey or basketball. You're doing a lot of the work yourself, and it's not a sport that earns you a high salary. You're not in it for the money. You can't be.

If you let those outside sources define you, you're setting yourself up to be let down. I've had my carding come and go, and there have been times that it's made me question whether or not I belong in this sport. But every time, I realize that it's a terrible waste to let someone else—someone who doesn't know everything about me, who only is looking at a small subset of numbers related to my results that season—dictate whether or not I'm an athlete. I'm persistent. If I hear a "no" now, I believe it can become a "yes" later... if I keep fighting for that dream.

Even in these moments of pause, where I'm working to come back from an injury and not able to push in the way I'd like to be, I stay persistent. The setback is a chance to focus on healing and strengthening, to come back even better. Every setback is a chance to learn something, as long as you're constantly trying to move through it and move forward. You didn't get carding? Fine. What do you need to do to get it for next season? How can you make it through until then financially? Are there grants? Do you need to use the offseason to add more part-time work? The only time a setback can truly set you back is when you allow yourself to stay stuck in that moment.

You also need to celebrate yourself when you do get a result, because they don't come along every day. After I broke the school record the first time, on the same day, another girl at another meet broke the 400-meter collegiate record and I remember a teammate coming over to tell me that. I'm sure she didn't mean anything by it, but it immediately made me feel less-than because suddenly, this record that I had been so proud of breaking just an hour ago felt like it wasn't as impressive.

Looking back, I'm furious that I let her derail my celebration. I felt like celebrating my record was cut short because the attention was being directed to someone who ran faster than me. Imposter Syndrome immediately stepped back in. I would have loved to just be in the moment, but my brain instantly sped up. All I could think was, 'Great, I broke the school record. But how much faster can I run? What should I have done in that race to be faster?'

One thing that I've learned even from writing this book was that, looking back, I never took the time to celebrate the things that did go well, and those are moments I'll never get back. If I *could* go back, I would have told my teammate. 'Wow, that's great for her that she broke the collegiate record. But I'm really proud of my success, and I'm going to celebrate this win for me.' I would have stood up for myself more and would have taken that moment to enjoy having the record. In fact, I'm sure she would have celebrated with me! Most of us have moments like that, whether it's getting the A on the test or winning the race or just feeling like you crushed your performance in the school play. Really see yourself for who you are, and for the accomplishments you've had. Give yourself space to recognize that and celebrate that. It's so important to look at your own journey as opposed to everyone else's.

As I was working on this book, I was healing from a tibia injury and really struggling to find answers. I was lucky enough to start working with a great physiologist right around the time we were finishing up the first draft of the book, and during one particularly painful session of needling, he was asking me about it. I told him a bit of the premise, and mentioned that a lot of what we were talking about was finding a sense of self, a sense of belonging, and leaving Imposter Syndrome behind.

Then, he asked me what Imposter Syndrome means. Instantly, three of the other women who were in the clinic at the time and I started offering him definitions. I thought it was so funny: he couldn't even conceptualize what it was, much less imagine having it. But I know he's in the minority. Most of us will deal with Imposter Syndrome throughout our lives, we just need to be able to identify it and move on from it faster.

And finally, what I hope you took from this book is that no

matter who you are, not every race will be a new personal best. No matter how hard you try, every race will come with different challenges, different stresses. When I had the expectation that every race, I should be running faster, I raced so much worse and I felt so much worse. When I was able to surrender to the reality that it's okay to *not* run faster every race, that's when I was able to make those small improvements over time.

The best races happen when I go out there believing I'm going to enjoy the race and I'm going to give it my best shot. I really love to compete. And I love to surprise myself. I'm not afraid to come back from behind and I'm not afraid to defy expectations of who I am. There's a balance between constantly striving for better results and faster times, while still celebrating the wins and accepting that these things take time.

Keep running.

ACKNOWLEDGMENTS

"MOST LIKELY TO WIN A GOLD MEDAL AT THE OLYMPICS goes to… Micha Powell!" I read the high school superlative that my peers voted on, and my first thought was, "I don't remember telling more than a handful of people of my plans of making the Olympics." I guess my actions spoke for themselves, even then.

I might not have a gold medal from the Olympics (yet), but I have achievements that would make my 18-year-old self so proud and more than anything, so happy in the way that I have showed up for myself over the years.

I would like to express my deepest appreciation to those who have made this ongoing track and field journey have far more blissful highs than heartache-inducing lows.

Mom: You are my rock! I know that if I ever need anything, you'll be right there. Whether that's as a coach, mentor, best friend or protector, your ability to make me feel unstoppable is one of your many superpowers. Thanks for choosing me to be your daughter.

Grandma: Thank you for always believing in me and for instilling my love of sport at such a young age. I cherish our long phone calls and your wisdom of being the most authentic version of yourself.

Bubs: To my love, I don't even know how to begin to thank you. David, you have kept me grounded in my truth. You are my gravity, keeping me centered and anchored to my purpose. Thank you for reminding me to celebrate the small wins too.

Coach V: Thank you for your unwavering support and encouragement throughout my track and field career. Thank you Coach V for reminding me that I don't have to be like anyone else to be extraordinary, but rather, I just need to focus on the strengths that I already possess and write my own path to success.

Molly Hurford: You are a wizard! Thank you for believing in my story. It has been incredible working with you on *Sprinting Through Setbacks*.

To my friends: Thank you to my people. Those who have known me before I started running track and those I met because of it, thank you for reminding me the importance of connection and self-love as we strive towards living our most meaningful lives.

ABOUT THE AUTHORS

MICHA POWELL

Micha Powell is a 2022 Commonwealth Games gold medalist and a world-class Canadian Olympic sprinter specializing in the 400 meter. Born in Montreal to 3x Olympian Rosey Edeh and Long Jump World Record Holder Mike Powell, athletics is a part of her DNA.

MOLLY HURFORD

Molly Hurford is a writer and podcaster in love with all things cycling, running, nutrition and movement-related. She's a little obsessed with getting people—especially women—psyched on adventure and being outside. She's written 10 books about endurance sport, including the *Shred Girls*, a middle grade fiction series focused on getting girls excited about bikes.

Find more books like this at StrongGirlPublishing.com

Printed in the USA
CPSIA information can be obtained
at www.ICGtesting.com
JSHW010933100724
66028JS00001B/7